THE PUFFIN JOKE BOOK

How this book happened:

It's been happening, actually, for ages, ever since I was at school, looking out of the window and learning illogical-rhymes (like Caesar and geezer) instead of logarithms, and not-sticking-to-dates and failing in Jography and passing on riddles. So naturally when it came to writing a book I was in the right position to do it (one ear to the ground, the other one pricked for the distant sound of jokes). At the same time it was a bit tricky.

Well, stuck like that, I couldn't read books (except Lewis Carroll) or get about much, so I used agents – like hundreds of Puffin Club members who posted riddles, and elephants who happened to drop in, and shaggy dogs and that sort of thing, not counting all the friends* who remembered stories (sometimes the same only different) and new riddles, and finished old rhymes for me, and Quentin Blake, who brought everything to life.

So when I finally straightened up, it was just a matter of setting the history books right on a few points, like the Battle of Waterloo, and Robert the Bruce, and wondering Why was the Dodo? What was the strange secret of the gravestone? What do alpacas do in Caracas? And putting the facts straight about parrots, and cannibal birds, and of course Uncle Bob . . .

And so it's happened. Or at least I think it has, unless some wretched joking person has left all the other pages blank! Just check, will you?

*Leslie Norris, Dave Brier, Andrew Cunningham, the children of Midhurst Grammar School, all members of the Puffin Club and lots of other people. Thank you.

BRONNIE CUNNINGHAM

The Puffin Joke Book

ILLUSTRATED BY
QUENTIN BLAKE

PUFFIN BOOKS

Puffin Books, Penguin Books Ltd, Harmondsworth, Middlesex, England
Viking Penguin Inc., 40 West 23rd Street, New York, New York 10010, U.S.A.
Penguin Books Australia Ltd, Ringwood, Victoria, Australia
Penguin Books Canada Limited, 2801 John Street, Markham, Ontario, Canada L3R 1B4
Penguin Books (N.Z.) Ltd, 182–190 Wairau Road, Auckland 10, New Zealand

—

Published in Puffin Books 1974
Reprinted 1974, 1975 (twice), 1976 (twice), 1977,
1978, 1979, 1980 (twice), 1981 (twice), 1983 (twice), 1984, 1985, 1986

—

Copyright © Bronnie Cunningham, 1974
Illustrations copyright © Quentin Blake, 1974
All rights reserved

—

Set, printed and bound in Great Britain by
Cox & Wyman Ltd, Reading
Set in Monotype Plantin

Designed by Treld Pelkey Bicknell

For Andrew, Dee, Euan, Patrick and Sandy

Yes, there's absolutely no doubt about it ...

(P.T.O.)

... it's a clear case of catastrophic gloombiges.

I shall have to put you on
the Puffin Joke Book *for a week . . .*

. . . it's kill or cure

Monday Limericks
OOPS! 'ERE WE GO!

There was an old dame of Nicaragua
Whose hair was clawed off by a jagua;
    When he saw 'twas a wig,
    He exclaimed, 'Now I twig,
What a false artificial old hagua.'

THE ABOMINABLE SNOWMAN

A SNOWMAN who lived in Tibet,
Bought some snow shoes, to keep out the wet.
    'They're the most,' he declared,
    'Peculiar, weird,
And ABOMINABLE shoes I could get.'

THE FOSSILIZED DINOSAUR

One day down the mine, an old miner saw
The bones of a fossilized dinosaur,
 Said he, 'This 'ere pick
 Is too clumsy and thick,
Just wait, and I'll get me a finer saw.'

*

OUR VICAR

He is really as mild as a lamb;
But when he sat down in the jam
 On taking his seat
 At our Sunday school treat,
We all heard our Vicar say – 'Stand up, please, while I say
 grace.'

*

AH, BEAUTIFUL FEATHERS
AND A HEART OF GOLD....

MODESTY WAS
NEVER HIS STRONG
POINT

Days of the Week

Cut them on Monday, you cut them for health;
Cut them on Tuesday, you cut them for wealth;
Cut them on Wednesday, you cut them for news;
Cut them on Thursday, a new pair of shoes;
Cut them on Friday, you cut them for sorrow;
Cut them on Saturday, see your true love tomorrow;
Cut them on Sunday, ill luck will be with you all the week.

You musn't sing on Sunday,
  Because it is a sin,
But you may sing on Monday,   *
  Till Sunday comes again.

Friday night's dream
  On Saturday told,
Is sure to come true,
  Be it ever so old.

Monday's child is fair of face,
Tuesday's child is full of grace,
Wednesday's child is full of woe,
Thursday's child has far to go,
Friday's child is loving and giving,
Saturday's child works hard for its living;
But the child that is born on the Sabbath Day
Is fair and wise and good and gay.

Solomon Grundy,
Born on a Monday,
Christened on Tuesday,
Married on Wednesday,
Took ill on Thursday,
Worse on Friday,
Died on Saturday,
Buried on Sunday;
That is the end
Of Solomon Grundy.

No. 1 Dr Schmoller's Portable Duck-pond

Don't leave your feathered friends behind when you go on holiday. The portable duck-pond provides your web-footed pets with a comfortable journey and an all-round view: and every turn of the central handle produces delightful waves.

Monday's Bird:
The Duck

IT'S WICKED

Ode on a duck's pond being his castle,
  and how he should stay there

The place   Mr Huddle
for a   Sitting in a puddle
duck   Green garters and
is a   yellow toes.
pond.   Tell me this riddle,
                   Or I'll smash your nose!

Not
the
wicket
at
cricket.

Who takes a gun under
his wing when he flies?
A hi-quacker.

*And when you see Monday coming it's no good
        ducking – JOIN SAM.*

What goes 'kcauq, kcauq'? A duck flying backwards.

What language is 'quack quack'? Double ducks.

Why can't a duck fly upside down? Because he'd quack up.

What do you get when you cross a duck with a cow? Cream quackers.

*

ISAY, ISAY, ISAY; WHAT IS THE DIFFERENCE BETWEEN A DUCK? ONE OF ITS LEGS IS BOTH THE SAME! I GIVE UP

Fowl and Beastly Jokes

How do you stop a cock crowing on Monday morning ?
Eat him for Sunday lunch.

What did the Spanish farmer say to his hen ?
Olé

What's small and hairy and has six legs ?
An ant with a fur coat on.

If a bird is run over by a lawn mower, what do you get ?
Shredded tweet.

What do hedgehogs eat for lunch ?
Prickled onions.

One day a gorilla, a bear, and a monkey were on a bus, when
the monkey said he wanted some toast. So the bear gave him
a slice of bread, and the monkey put it under the gorilla
(griller).

And how do you milk a hedgehog?

VERY CAREFULLY.

What do you get when you pour boiling water down a rabbit-hole?

A hot cross bunny.

What do you get when you cross a bear with a kangaroo?

A fur coat with big pockets.

An Australian was showing a man from Texas round his farm one day. He pointed out his cows. 'Why,' said the Texan, 'back home we have pigs as big as those.' He showed him his sheep. 'Why,' said the Texan, 'back home we've got cats bigger than that.' And then a kangaroo came hopping by. 'Say,' called the Texan, 'but you sure have fine big grasshoppers out here.'

*

I'D TELL YOU THE ONE ABOUT THE GIANT DOUGHNUT, BUT YOU'D NEVER SWALLOW IT.

Mick and Mulligan

Some of my best friends are lunatics – but the nuts I really like best are Mick and Mulligan, especially when they get talking together . . .

      MICK: How high is a Chinaman, Mulligan?
MULLIGAN: About five foot?
      MICK: No, how high is a Chinaman?
MULLIGAN: Five foot one, then?
      MICK: No, Mulligan. How Hi is a Chinaman.

. . . and it's just ridiculous to put up with Mondays week after week.
JOIN SAM.

MICK: Have you heard of the man who fell ill one day with a terrible pain in his stomach? They opened him up in hospital, and inside him they found 258 things that he'd swallowed. There was a 3 lb. piece of metal, 26 keys, 3 sets of rosary beads, 16 religious medals, a bracelet, a necklace, 3 pairs of tweezers, 4 nail clippers, 39 nail files, and 88 assorted coins. And it's true as I'm standing here. What do you think of that?

MULLIGAN: Ah, to be sure, and that's a strange thing. But maybe you haven't heard about my old gran?

MICK: What happened to her?

MULLIGAN: Well, we was in the kitchen, and first of all the old lady bolted the door – and then I told her a story with 57 rhinoceroses, 25 rare white elephants, a grand piano, 1,985 white ants, a porcupine, 3 lobsters, a saucepan, the express train from London to Manchester, and 16 hairpins in it – and, bless me, if she didn't swallow it whole!

MICK: That must have been a rare story, Mulligan. How did it go?

MULLIGAN: Well, it was like this . . .

(*And then the telephone rang and I had to answer it . . .*)

Riddles of History Answered

What happened AFTER King John lost everything in the Wash?

The East Anglian Wash Company
Kings Lynnen

Dear Sire,

With reference to your complaint. We can find no trace of the crown, sceptre, etc., which you say we lost.

Were these clearly marked with your name and address? I'm afraid we cannot accept responsibility for anonymous treasures.

Perhaps you had really lost them before coming here?

We have, however, found one item which appears to be marked with your name. This is a large piece of paper. Is this important? If so, and you will give us your new address, we would be glad to forward it to you.

> We were, Sire,
> Your obedient servants,
>
> The East Anglian Wash Company

Missing - on Monday

NOTICE

Will the person who took my ladder on Sunday morning please return it, or further steps will be taken.

THE CASE OF THE EIGHT
STOLEN WATCHES

A report came into Witsend Police Station at 9 a.m. on Monday morning. A jeweller's shop had been broken into. Eight watches had been stolen.

So they called in Sergeant Duffer. Now Duffer may *sound* stupid, and he looks a bit of a nut, but he's got a razor-sharp brain hidden under that big helmet of his. (They discovered that when he'd gone through three helmets in four weeks – cut to ribbons.)

Sergeant Duffer went down to investigate.

'Hello, hello, helloo,' said the Sergeant. 'Someone's nicked eight watches out of the window, but he's left about fifty behind. H'm. *And* he's broken eight panes of glass to do it. Now that's very significacious, *that* is.'

And before you could say knife (or razor, even) Sergeant Duffer knew who he was looking for. And he got him. Who was it?

Answer: Number 1 at the end of the book.

＊

How does an intruder get into the house?
Intruder the window!

Munday's Punday

YOU'LL HAVE TO
GO EASY ON THE
CAKE-CRUMBS
FOR A BIT...

What do you give a sick bird?   Tweetment.

What's the smell of bad eggs?   Extinct.

What's the expression on an auctioneer's face?   For bidding.

When did the Chinaman go to the dentist?   Two-thirty.

What do mice do in the day-time?   Mousework.

What do cats read?   Mews of the World.

Sentenced !

A man lay spread-eagled on the pavement, one Monday morning. He'd been knocked down by a car, shot in the arm, his cheek was cut from the fall, and blood was pouring from a gash in his leg.

Eventually a policeman came up, and bending over him, said, 'Have an accident, sir ?'

But the man replied, 'No thanks, I've had one already.'

'Well,' said the policeman, 'there's a hospital just down the road. I'll just get a car to run you down.'

But the man replied, 'No thanks, I've had one already.'

When he got to the hospital, they took out the bullet, bandaged his leg, and stitched up his cheek. After all that, he asked the nurse for a cigarette.

'It's darned cheek!' retorted the nurse, 'but you can have one if you like.'

But the man replied, 'No thanks, I've had one already.'

When the man was quite ready to leave hospital, the doctor saw him, to give his final report. The doctor looked up from a sheaf of papers and said, 'It says here that your progress has been excellent. Perhaps you'd like the bulletin ?'

But the man replied, 'No thanks, I've had one already.'

He finally went back to work. His arm was in a sling, his leg still wrapped in bandages, and his face was covered in sticking plaster. 'Good heavens,' said one of his mates, 'You've certainly been in the wars. I'd ask for a lot of damages, if I were you.'

But the man replied, 'No thanks, I've had one lot already, and that's *quite* enough.'

Died on Monday

To the Memory

of

JOHN FORBES

GAMBLER

He was not good
He was better

The Mystery of the Monk's Cold Feet

A very tall young Englishman went to live in a monastery in Ireland, to learn to be a monk.

He got used to the life after a while, but there was one thing he just couldn't bear. His feet were always cold.

You see, he was so tall, that when he lay on his bunk at night, the blanket (and there was only one) just wouldn't stretch as far as his toes.

Finally, the old monk in the cell next door, said to him:

'You'll need to be cutting a yard of your blanket off of the top, and be adding it to the bottom.'

Cut a yard off the top, and add it to the bottom?!

The Englishman thought the old Irish monk must be barmy. What do you think?

Answer: Number 2 at the end of the book.

What has four legs, one head and a foot?
    A bed.
What has four legs and flies?
    Two pairs of trousers.
What has four legs and feathers?
    A featherbed.

This   =   That

A nice poem	*An ice poem*
You sing	Using
I sing	icing
sugar	sugar
ikon	I can
ice a	ice a
bun.	bun.
I sand	Ice and
milk or	milk, or
I saw	ice, or
water	water-
I scan	ice can
make	make
I screams.	ice-creams.

SARDINES ON
SEAWEED FOR
TEA

WHAT A VERY
BEAUTIFUL THOUGHT

*I'm stopping in here till it's all
safely over.*

Q. What is it that you want, but when you have it you don't
know that you have it ?
    A. Sleep.
Q. What is lower with a head on it than without one ?
    A. A pillow.
Q. What can it be ? The greater it is, the less you see of it ?
    A. Darkness.
Q. What is more terrifying, the smaller it is ?
    A. A bridge.
Q. What is it that I can see but you cannot ?
    A. The back of your head.
Q. You use it between your head and toes.
    The more it works, the thinner it grows.
        A. A bar of soap.

✳

I'm not sure that Monday is all that wonderful.

I think it's absolutely TERRIBLE.

It's Just Riddliculous!

How do you hire a horse?
    Put four bricks under it.

What do you always see running along the streets in town?
    Pavements.

How many sexes are there?
    Three. Male sex, female sex, and insects.

Why is it dangerous to have a nap in a railway compartment?
    Because the train runs over sleepers.

Why do women put their hair in rollers at night?
    So they can wake curly in the morning.

Why do wizards drink tea?
    Because sorcerers need cuppas.

If buttercups are yellow, what colour are hiccups?

> Burple.

When is longhand quicker than shorthand?

> When it's on a clock.

What was the largest island before Australia was discovered?

> Australia.

How did Hiawatha?

> With thoap and water.

Why do heroes wear big shoes?

> Because of their amazing feats.

THE DAY THE LIGHTNING STRUCK

The vicar took one Monday morning off, and went down to the club to play golf. He met Sam Green there, and they set off together to play a game.

Now the vicar was quite good at golf. But Sam Green wasn't, and he was having a very bad day. He just couldn't get the ball into the hole. Every time he had to make a putt, he missed. And every time, he said, 'Damn. Missed.'

The vicar was getting a bit upset by this. At last he said, 'I say, Green, do you mind not swearing.' But at the very next hole Green aimed from only two feet away, and the ball went past. 'Damn. Missed,' he said.

The vicar was really put out this time. 'Look here, Green, if you swear again, God will hear you, and strike you dead with lightning.' Green tried very hard at the next hole. He spent ages looking at the ball, and moving leaves away from the grass, and practising shots. Finally, he hit the ball very gently, and it stopped just two inches from the hole. 'Damn. Missed,' cried Sam Green. And the heavens opened. There was a tremendous crack of thunder. A flash of lightning shot down from the sky, and hit the vicar.

Then a deep voice came from on high. 'Damn. Missed.'

Join Sam

Who's SAM? SAM is the Society for Abolishing Monday.

What's he doing? He's trying to GET RID OF MONDAY.

How? SAM's plan is simple. (It's simply the best idea since ice cream.) In future there will be LEAP WEEKS, like Leap Years. This means that, except in August, the week will go

STRAIGHT FROM SUNDAY TO TUESDAY!

There will be *no more Monday Mornings* ever again.

It's just common sense. When you think of all those centuries of Monday mornings that no one's ever wanted – why should we put up with them any more? A little clear thinking and – whoof – they're gone for ever. (Like slavery and thumb-screws.)

As SAM says: What a short step, from Sunday to Tuesday, but what a giant LEAP for mankind!

Do you think I'm joking? Don't be too sure. Stranger things have happened . . .

JOIN SAM

Teeth

What's worse than a giraffe with a sore throat, or a millipede with sore feet?

A crocodile with toothache.

Why does my grandmother have such a high-pitched voice?
Because of her falsetto teeth.

What's the best thing to
put into pies?
Your teeth.

She went to the pictures
     tomorrow,
And took a front seat at the
     back.
She put her false teeth in her
     handbag,
And her tongue it went
     clickety clack.

*I declare that
this is the
tooth, the whole
tooth, and
nothing but the
tooth.*

We knocked on a lot of doors on Tuesday, because we were out asking questions for the Bronnie Opinion Poll (BOP). And we met a lot of people. But when we left our questionnaire for them to fill up – it wasn't so good.

We asked: 'What do you think of Tuesday?'

On the whole we drew a blank.

←

5% of the answers came back through the window – as paper darts.

Two dustmen returned 12%.

One parrot came into the office personally, and said 'Pretty Poll,' but when we said 'How about Tuesday?' he got shy and flew away.

Only two people sent back the forms with a proper answer. 50% of those said they liked it, and 50% said they didn't. So we called it a draw.

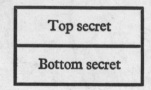

| Top secret |
| Bottom secret |

Drawing of 2 drawers by 1 drawer.

*

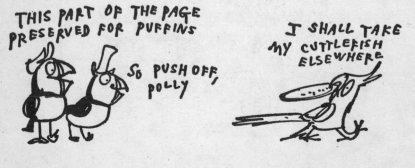

THIS PART OF THE PAGE PRESERVED FOR PUFFINS

SO PUSH OFF, POLLY

I SHALL TAKE MY CUTTLEFISH ELSEWHERE

Actually, most people were too busy down the road, waiting outside the window of Miss Marshall's laundry shop. Want to know why?

Miss Marshall has two sun-blinds over her shop window. (She sells hand-knitted garments as well as doing laundry.) And right across these two blinds she has a message written.

But this Tuesday morning was very grey and cloudy, so she only had the right blind down.

NO. I
MISS MAR SHALL
FRENCH LA UNDRESS
EVERYTHING FOR SALE IN THIS WINDOW
LAUNDRY RECEIVED EACH MORNING
WILL BE RETURNED PUNCTUALLY
NEXT DAY AT 12 O'CLOCK

And when Miss Marshall looked out at 12 o'clock, a huge crowd was jamming the pavement outside.

AND HOW'S BUSINESS ON TUESDAY, THEN?

Tailor	Just sew-sew.
Electrician	It's pretty light.
Farmer	Mine is growing.
Dustman	It's picking up.
Refrigerator salesman	Not so hot.
Astronomer	It's looking up.
Lift operator	It has its ups and downs.
Optician	It's looking better.
Author	Mine is all write!

✳ ✳ ✳

Knock, Knock.
Who's there?
Howard.
Howard who?
Howard you like to be outside
     for a change?

Knock, Knock.
Who's there?
Major.
Major who?
Major answer, didn't I?

Knock, Knock.
Who's there?
Felix.
Felix who?
Felix my ice-cream,
   I'll lick his.

Knock, Knock.
Who's there?
Havelock.
Havelock who?
Havelock and key
   put on the door

Knock, Knock.
Who's there?
Mahatma.
Mahatma who?
Mahatma coat, please.

Knock, Knock.
Who's there?
Signor.
Signor who?
Signor light on.

Knock, Knock.
Who's there?
Mr.
Mr who?
Missed her at the bus-stop.

Knock, Knock,
Who's there?
Ivan.
Ivan who?
Ivan idea.
You've an idea what?
Ivan idea
   – it's me.

Knock, Knock.
Who's there?
BOO!
Boo-hoo?
Don't cry, it's only a joke.

And shall I tell you the story about the red-hot poker? No – you'd never be able to grasp it!

Can I have Just One Word
with you please?

Just one word will fill the gaps in each rhyme, but you need to change the letters round (e.g. gnat, tang).

A . . . old woman
On . . . bent
Put on her . . .
And away she went.
'Come, . . . my son,'
She was heard to say,
'Who shall we . . .
Upon today?'

'I like to . . .,'
Said wicked Tom,
Throw a brick, or . . .;
Maybe a bomb.

And when the fun
Is getting . . .
At . . . I know
I'll land in gaol!'

vile, evil, veil, Levi, live

steal, slate, stale, least

I went to the Palace
The other day,
To see the . . .
At work and play.
They let off . . .
In every way,
'Well, . . .,' I said,
You earn your pay.'

These gaps are all the same
word.
Jack Brown one day
A . . . falls down,
And tears . . . in his eyes.
'. . . bless my boots,'
Says old Jack Brown,
'I will get . . . , not die.'

teams, steam, mates
(At Crystal Palace ground!)

well

Tuesday's Limericks

There was an Arabian Sheik,
Who entered his harem and speik,
  'A loud cry I heard,
  And in here it occurred,
Are my fifty-two children aweik?'

There was a young lady called Wemyss,
Who, it semyss, was troubled with dremyss.
   She would wake in the night
   And, in terrible fright,
Shake the bemyss of the house with her scremyss.

*

There once was a canner so canny
Who remarked with a smile to his granny,
   'A canner can can
   Anything that he can,
But a canner can't can a can, can he?'

A crazy young rebel called Tom,
Started fooling about with a bomb.
   They got most of him up
   With a teaspoon and cup,
And returned him by post, to his momb.

There once was a dashing young mouse
Who was bored with only one spouse.
   'I think one more wife,
   Would add spice to my life,
And be nicer to have round the house.'

Tuesday's Bird: The Parrot

GOOD-MORNING, PARROTS

Tell me,
how do you greet
A cockatoo and a parakeet?
Do you say
Good Day –
or How do you do,
To a Parakeet and a Cockatoo?

Do you say
Hello, *so* pleased to meet,
Mr Cockatoo and Miss Parakeet?

And when you go,
Do you say, Hello,
It's time to fly –
Or just, Good-bye,
Or Toodle-oo
Miss Parakeet,
Mr Cockatoo?

GREETINGS
O PARROTS!

Man: 'Can I have a parrot for my son, please?'
Pet-shop owner: 'Sorry sir, we don't swop.'

Looking After Parrots

BY L. O. POLL

First of all – look *before* you get your parrot. Look for one in a cage. If it's in a glass case, don't buy it, it's stuffed.

And get ear-plugs at the same time. You never know, you might be unlucky and buy a *politician** by mistake – talking in *polysyllables* all the time. If you have got one of those, the only thing to do is keep him shut up as much as possible.

Now for feeding. The best thing is *polyfilla*. I think *polystyrene* is a bit too solid for everyday, so keep it for a treat on Chewsdays.

And do remember to give your parrot love and care as

well. A parrot's cage should be a real home to him, never a *polycell*.

Give him a holiday once in a while. Try taking him to *Polynesia* sometimes – or if that's too far, twice round the garden will have to do.

Of course, he may escape, and that's *polygon*, isn't it? Just let him go. A lot of people have done themselves a serious injury (like cricks in the neck) from looking after parrots when they've flown away.

The thing to do then, is go to the nearest *Polytechnic* and learn a bit more about them – *parrot-fashion*.

Or there's always the zoo.

*A Poly-Titian is quite different – that's valuable.

The Parrot and the Conjuror

Have you heard about the conjuror, who used to entertain the passengers every night on board ship?

Well, every night, he gave his show, and every time he did, a parrot used to sit not far away, with his beady eyes fixed on him.

And when the conjuror hid a card up his sleeve, the parrot would croak: 'It's up his sleeve.' And when he slipped a rabbit in his pocket, the parrot would croak: 'Down his trousers, down his trousers.'

The conjuror was dying to wring his neck.

But one night, when the conjuror was in the middle of his tricks, the ship hit an iceberg, broke in two, and sank almost immediately. The conjuror found himself in the water and thrashed about to keep afloat, until he eventually managed to pull himself up on to an empty raft. He flopped on to it, absolutely exhausted. And who should be perched on the far edge of the raft too? The parrot. And the parrot's beady eyes were fixed on the conjuror.

The conjuror just lay there, flat out, for nearly an hour. And all the while the parrot never stirred, and he never for one second took his eyes off the conjuror.

Finally, the conjuror moved, and opened his eyes. And the parrot croaked: 'Alright, I give up. Where's the ship?'

*

I'D TELL YOU THE ONE ABOUT THE NEW ROOF, BUT IT'S WAY, OVER YOUR HEAD.

Knock Knock, who's there?
Mick and Mulligan

MICK: I can make you talk like an Indian.
MULLIGAN: O.K., go ahead.
MICK: I can make you talk like an Indian.
MULLIGAN: How?
MICK: There you are.

MICK: How do you pronounce FOLK?
MULLIGAN: Folk.
MICK: How do you pronounce the white of an egg?
MULLIGAN: Yoke.
MICK: Have you ever eaten a meringue, Mulligan?

Tuesday Puzzles

MA'S A GRAN!

Anagrams are no joke – or at least they used not to be. The monks of the Middle Ages, for instance, took them very seriously indeed.

What they did was this. They took some vital phrase from the Bible, made an anagram of the letters, and thought this revealed some great hidden truth.

For example: Pilate said to Jesus, 'What is truth?' Now in Latin, this is 'Quid est veritas?'

They twisted this round, and came up with the answer, '*Est vir qui adest*' – which means 'It is the man before you'! Abracadabra. Very convenient! I dread to think how many hours they must have wasted on all this – there are an awful lot of words in the Bible.

But don't worry, these aren't serious . . .

1. A chain of mountains will appear
    If you the name transpose
   Of those who were in ancient days
    Britain's piratic foes.
2. Can you make one word from the letters of NEW DOOR?
3. Cato and Chloe combined well together
   Make a very good drink for very bad weather.
4. Can you make just one word from these letters?
   DEJNOORSTUW
5. NINE THUMPS will give you this.

Riddles of History Answered

What did the spider say to Robert the Bruce?

Dear Robert the Bruce,

I just had to drop you a wee line or two, because I ken ye was worrit?

I'm ever sae baithered I never got to speak to ye, but there I was at a loose end, without a care in the worrrld – and when I stoppit, ye was oop and awa, as if the Deil himself was at yer heels.

Now, I've been spinning webs sin auld lang syne, and there's nowt easier than that. So, tak the worrrd of a canny Scot – dinna fash yerself. Whatever it is, if ye canna do it, ye canna do it, and that's all there is t'it. So, tak it easy, mon. Relax.

That's the wee piece of advice I was wanting to tell ye. I hope I'm not too late?

Jest Animals

I wonder why
the armadillo
stuffs a
pillow,
and iguanas
munch bananas?

The gnu knows,
If ewe don't.

Why does a donkey eat thistles?
    Because he's an ass!

What kind of sound irritates an oyster?
    A noisy noise annoys an oyster.

What do bees do with all their honey?
    They cell it.

What do you get if you cross a jeep with a dog?
    A land rover.

What happens when a horse gets to the bottom of his
nosebag?
    It's the last straw!

What's grey, and has four legs and a trunk?
A mouse going on holiday.

What's brown and has four legs and a trunk?
A mouse coming back from holiday.

*

TONGUE TWISTER

This is the shortest, but I promise you it's the worst of all.
The sixth sick sheik's sixth sheep's sick.
(Of course you have to say it very fast, at least six times.)

A SHICK SEETH'S KEITHSCHLICK...
A SHLEETH'S KICK STUCK...
A SNICK TEETH'S TUCK SMICK.....

NOT BAD, NOW
TRY SAYING IT
QUICKLY

UNCLE BOB

My Uncle Bob's a careful man,
He's always dressed just so.
His waistcoat's always buttoned,
And his shoes – they always glow.

He wears a fancy patterned tie,
His hair is slick and trim,
His socks are best Bri-nylon,
And his trousers – very slim.

Now every day he takes his gun,
He's very fond of it;
He thinks it goes with his smart clothes,
But he's *never* scored a hit!

One day he went to Africa,
To have a shooting gala.
He tracked the tricky rhino –
Nearly shot a swift impala.

He followed all the antelope
On foot, and very hot
Upon the trail of elephants,
He peppered them with shot.

But in the wild and lurid bush,
One hot and sticky day,
He came upon a shaggy beast –
Completely blocked his way.

It leaped upon poor Uncle Bob
And stripped him at one go.

It tore his buttoned waistcoat,
And it gnawed the shoes which glow.

It chewed upon the fancy tie,
It clawed the hair so trim;
It ate his best Bri-nylon socks,
But it didn't fancy him.

The shaggy beast, well satisfied,
Went for a quiet lie-down.
Poor Bob, quite nude, and most subdued,
Limped, gun in hand, to town.

Where he was arrested for

Being in unlawful possession of firearms,
Unseemly behaviour,
Carrying an offensive weapon,
Indecent exposure,
And Causing a breach of the peace.

THE DODO

The dodo had a cold in its nose,
Or rather, its beak,
And could hardly speak.

When a man said,
'I thought you were dead,'
Said the dodo,
'Oh dodo,
I've just got a code id de head.'

So maybe the dodo
Was really a
Yes-yes,

Or could be a
Nono?

USEFUL INVENTIONS OF DAYS GONE BY

HE USED TO GET SO CHILLY ON WINTER EVENINGS

No. 2 The Knitted Parrot-Cosy

The parrot-cosy was first developed by Dame Florence Bugloss, the animal-lover and philanthropist, for her own parrot, Lucifer. She also devised a set of tartan slippers for a Newfoundland dog.

Riddlology

What's the best place for water-skiing ¿
> A lake with a slope.

If an Indian woman is a squaw, what's an Indian baby?
> A squawker.

What's the first thing to take when you're run down?
> The number of the car.

What can be right but never wrong?
> An angle.

What happens to a boy when he misses the last bus home?
> He catches it when he gets back.

What is black and comes out of the ground shouting 'Knickers, knickers'?
> Crude oil.

And what comes out of the ground shouting 'Underwear, underwear'?
> Refined oil.

What's the best way of preventing seasickness?
> Bolt your food down.

Why was the patient's cough better in the morning?
> He'd been practising all night!

And have you heard this?

Spring is sprung
De grass is riz,
I wonder where de boidies is?

De boid is on the wing.
But dat's absoid,
I always thought
De wing was on de boid.

Food on Tuesday

MAN: 'Waiter, there's a cockroach nibbling my meat.'
WAITER: 'Don't worry, sir. They've got very small appetites.'

MAN: 'Waiter, I'd like some fish please.'
WAITER: 'Just a moment, sir, and I'll lay a plaice.'

MAN: 'I want a really good dinner. What do you recommend?'
WAITER: 'The Cozy Café round the corner, sir.'

MAN: 'Waiter, there's a caterpillar in my cabbage.'
WAITER: 'It's alright, sir. There's no extra charge.'

MAN: 'Waiter, there's a hair in my soup.'
WAITER: 'So sorry, sir. Did you order it without?'

MAN: 'I say, why are there double yellow lines round the menu?'
MANAGER: 'There's No Waiting here, sir. This is a self-service restaurant.'

WAITER: 'And what will you have, sir ?'
MAN: 'Steak and kiddly pie, please.'
WAITER: 'You mean steak and *kidney*, sir.'
MAN: 'I said Kiddly, diddle I ?'

*

CHARLIE

Charlie Jones was a moth, and he lived in a carpet ware-house in Cardiff. And he was a very very special moth, because he was World Champion carpet-eater. Charlie had been World Champion for two years, and soon the Championships were coming round again, and he was *determined* to win once more.

Charlie trained very hard before the match. Every day he went ten times across the ceiling of the carpet warehouse, and ten times down the far side, ten times he ate his way through the carpets stacked on the floor, and ten times he went up the wall again. After all that he felt pretty good, and when the time for the Championship match came, he went up to London feeling pretty sure of himself.

There were quite a lot of other moths contending for the title, and each moth had to eat through various different kinds of carpets – Welsh, Persian, Turkish, Chinese, Axminster, Wilton. Whoever ate through all these in the fastest time would be the Champion. The moths were lined up – the whistle went, and they were off.

Charlie started on the Welsh carpet, and his time was by far the best. Then he was on to the Persian, and again he held his lead. But by the time he had got to the Turkish carpet, he was being overhauled, by the moth on his left. This was the great Hiram C. Peabody, the American champion. Charlie was afraid of Hiram C. Peabody. He'd heard that Hiram had got a new trainer, with new methods. And it was beginning to show. Hiram was overtaking him.

Through the Chinese and the Axminster they nibbled like fury. The race was now between Charlie and Hiram – the rest were nowhere. And as they neared the end of the Wilton, Charlie just couldn't keep up. Hiram inched ahead, and the Championship was his.

And now it was poor Charlie's turn, as ex-Champion, to present the Carpet Cup to his hated rival, Hiram C. Peabody. Charlie stood on the rostrum with the Cup in his hands, and he couldn't bear it. In full view of everybody, he began to cry – and then he began to sob – and finally be broke down completely, and he started to bawl.

And Charlie found himself, suddenly, quite alone, with the Cup in his hands. And Hiram C. Peabody never came back to collect it. Why? Well you know what moth-balls are, don't you?

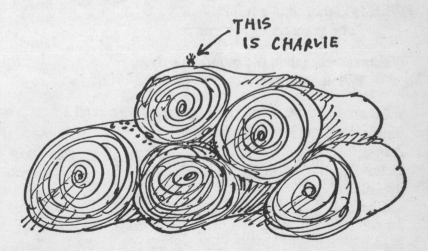

THIS
IS CHARLIE

Things Ain't What They Seem!

I saw a pack of cards gnawing a bone
I saw a dog seated on Britain's throne
I saw the Queen shut up in a box
I saw an orange driving a fat ox
I saw a butcher not a fortnight old
I saw a greatcoat all of solid gold
I saw two buttons talking of their lives
I saw my friends who told it to their wives

(Foxed? Try a comma in the middle of the lines.)

OLD IRISH FANCIES

Two fences of stone, two pools of water, two human
graves, and two bunches of rushes. What are they?
Teeth, eyes, nostrils, eyebrows.

What cannot God make?
Two hills without a valley between them.

What is higher than a hill?
The grass that grows on it.

What is smaller than the mouth of a fly?
What goes into it.

What are the three things that are never seen at all?
An edge, wind, and love.

How long will it be until speech comes to the rook?
When the eagles shall forsake the glens,
And the fog shall depart from the hills,
When the priest shall lose greed,
Speech shall come to the rook.

LIEUTENANT POTTS

Lieutenant Jeremiah Potts was my great-uncle on my mother's side. He was very old when I knew him. (I think he was the only retired Lieutenant in the British Army.)

He'd been quite distinguished, too, when he was *in* the Army. No one knew whether Lieutenant Potts was really potty (well, *I* know he wasn't), or a rotten radio-operator, or just couldn't spell, but some very odd messages got sent back to Headquarters when he was at the front.

The sergeant brought one in to Major Mountjoy. 'From Lieutenant Potts, sir,' he said, smirking somewhat.

Major Mountjoy looked it over. This is what it said.

'SEND THREE AND FOURPENCE. I AM GOING TO A DANCE.'

'Got any ideas, Sergeant ?' he said, more in sorrow than in anger.

'Yes, sir, certainly, sir.'

'SEND REINFORCEMENTS. I AM GOING TO ADVANCE.'

'Well, get on with it,' roared the Major.

And then there was the time he was *supposed* to be looking after the embarking of some men at the port, and sending them up the coast. Major Mountjoy was waiting – hoping to get some news.

The news came. It was the sergeant who brought in Pott's telegram, and waited for the explosion.

Major Mountjoy read it out:

'HAVE FOUND SOME FISH AND CHIPS. PLEASE SEND A DISH AND ALL MEN.'

'We'd better do what he says, eh what ?' said the Major sarcastically.

'Oh yes, sir.'

'I suppose *you* know what it means ?'

'Of course, sir. I rather think, sir, that Lieutenant Potts has found SUFFICIENT SHIPS and wants us to send ADDITIONAL MEN – I think sir.'

'Well, get on with it man,' roared the Major. If there was one thing he didn't like, more than stupid lieutenants, it was clever sergeants.

THE STORY OF HENRY ASS

Once upon a time there was an Ass called Henry. He was very keen on carrots and thistles, and all kinds of other assorted things, especially if they began with AS or ASS.

Can you finish his story for him, by filling in the blanks with words beginning as . . . or ass . . . ?

One day Henry climbed to the very top of a church steeple, and sat there. Why? Because he . . . to be good, and besides he liked the view. But the police, who took a different view, took him to court, and he was had up at the . . ., where they made him feel very small.

Why did you do it? they asked.

'I made the . . .,' Henry . . ., 'because I'm an . . . and that was the nearest I could get to the stars.' He wrote it all down on the form . . . to him.

The court . . . his case, and considered its verdict. They tore his character to shreds, and kicked him out, to boot, so poor old Henry had to . . . himself together again. 'After all,' he thought, 'it's not as if I was a real criminal, like an . . . I'm just a silly ass, and there's no harm in that.'

And after that he lived a long and happy life, until he died, when they wrote on his tombstone '. . . you were.'

A. aspired; Assizes; ascent; asserted; astronomer; assigned; assessed; assemble; assassin; Ass you were (or perhaps H. ass been?)

65

Bring your fiends

WITCHES

At Home and Abroad
on Witch Wednesday Night

All Kinds of Demon-strations

Phantom-weight Boxing Contest

Unlucky Dip ★ *Wizard Prizes*

Dress: Black eye and tails   8–12   Spirits served

(It's all white for ghosts)   R.I.P.

If you would like to know what you're invited to . . .

See opposite page

I think she must be going to a fancy-dress ball.

A GRAND OPEN-AIR SUPERNATURAL SPECTACULAR ANTI-SOCIAL

PROGRAMME

8.30 Black cat show
9.00 Sports will be held – bad sports will be let go
9.30 Red Devils sky-diving exhibition
10.00 Spitfire flying by the Dragons
11.00 Setting the impolite
12.00 Grand witches' fly-past

The Impossible Band will be playing tricks all evening.

MENU

Devilled Chickens, Deadly Nightshade - Cups of Tea
(bring your own sorcerers)

EXHIBITION OF ARTS AND WITCHCRAFTS

SKELETONS WILL BE SELLING RATTLE TICKETS

NO SPIRITS WILL BE SERVED AFTER HOURS

ENTRANCE FEE – YOUR MONEY AND YOUR LIFE

When's Day's Dinner
or
Can You Spell? Part Won

'Of coarse,' said the witch, roughly speaking, as usual. 'Witch spell do you want? That's the point,' fingering the sharp edge of her nife.

'Come ear, you,' she went on, grabbing holed of Tom as he went passed, and tweaking it. 'Call for my calldron. And where's my wond?'

Tom, who was her young son, but learning to a sister, got them both.

'Write then,' said the witch, and settling herself on the floor of the cave, she blue all the lights out. A terrible sneer parsed a cross her face.

'We must have a hire figher,' she screamed. 'We must have sticks and glue and wood you be kind enough,' here she grinned horribly at Tom, 'to tickle the toeds. Make sure there's a hot steak redy, rare and oozing, and dripping with blood, to poke their i's out with.'

'There aren't any i's in toads,' said Tom mildly.

'Then fetch an enormous big-toed monster, you jackassanapes,' she hissed, 'with hundreds of eyes.'

'There's only one eye in an enormous big-toed monster.'

'Then I will make one more,' shouted the witch exultantly, stirring the steaming calldron with her hands without paws.

'And what's next?' enquired Tom.

'Look on the menu, you gooseberry fool, look on the menu,' snarled the witch. 'There's snake and pygmy, and liver and dead, and muttering and tork, and hearts and rumps, and lights and heavywaits, and adders and multipliers, and ants and in sex, and beatles and spied hers, and p's in a pint, and buckets of blood, and yokes of eggs and whites of eyes – and eyes and i's, don't leave out the i's.' And the calldron seethed and bubbled and the witch seethed and fumed.

'What next?' asked Tom.

'Next?' said the witch, and waited a second and a third before continuing.

'Yes?' said Tom.

'Next,' she said, 'it's U.'

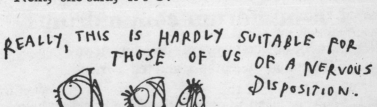

REALLY, THIS IS HARDLY SUITABLE FOR THOSE OF US OF A NERVOUS DISPOSITION.

(Did Tom go into the calldron ? Was he really on the menu ?
Read all about it in the next install meant – later in this book.)

Un-humdrum conumdrums

What are the quickest ways of spreading news ?
       Telephone, telegraph, and tell-a-friend.

What do you call an Eskimo with twelve balaclava helmets on ?
       You can call him anything, because he won't hear you.

Who invented the sewing-machine?
    Some clever sew-and-sew.

What's the difference between a well-dressed man and a tired dog?
    The man wears a suit, the dog just pants.

How can a man fall off a fifty-foot ladder and not be hurt?
    By falling off the bottom rung.

Why did the chicken cross the road?
    To get to the bird's eye shop.

What's the best way to remove paint from a chair?
    Sit down on it before it's dry.

What's a baby cow called?
    Condensed milk.

What's the difference between a crazy rabbit and a forged pound note?
    One is a mad bunny, and the other is bad money.

BLACK CAT AND MOUSE

There's a mouse
In my house.
It's nice –
For the mice.

They nibble and nobble
With whiskers a-wobble,
And they eat and they eat
   and they eat.

But There's a cat on the mat
   In my house.
   And that's dangerous,
      that.

   He jumps and he leaps,
   He can curl up in heaps,
   And he's going to eat,

He's going to eat
The mouse
In the house.

   Oh, how nice to have
     mice
   Thinks the cat,
   And that's dangerous,
      that.

scatter, patter
shiver, quiver

                bait – wait
                brood – food
            flash
      dash
            nip
      tip
        paw
        claw

        jaw

        munch
        crunch

        lunch

There's a mouse
In my house
On a mat

In a cat.

*

THE CAD!

THE BOUNDER!

JUST OFF TO
LOOK UP THE
ANSWERS
AT THE
BACK...

Riddles of History Answered

Who said Charles II could hide in the oak tree?

The Council Offices,
Little Under Wallop

To Charles Stuart,
London

Dear Sir,

It has been brought to our notice that you spent a night near this village in an unauthorized camping site – viz., an oak tree.

Permission for camping in the open can only be obtained from this office, for the special sites shown under Section 4, Rule 3, sub-section IVa. Horse parking is free. (Toilets will be installed as soon as they are invented.)

My Council will not tolerate long-haired layabouts coming down from London, causing pollution of the countryside, getting into fights, and disturbing the peace.

The fine for this offence is half-a-crown, plus half-a-crown for administrative costs.

Yours unfaithfully,

A. Yeoman
(Clerk to the Council)

P.S. The Divine Right of Kings does *not* apply to oak trees, and *certainly not* to Little Under Wallop.

THIS IS A DROODLE

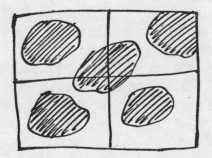

What is it?

A giraffe going past a window

Mental Arithmetic (very!)

1. If you add a father, a mother, and a baby, what do you get?

2. In one corner of a field there are $7\frac{3}{4}$ haystacks; in the second corner there are 30 haystacks; in the third corner $2\frac{1}{7}$ haystacks; in the fourth corner $1\frac{2}{7}$ hay stacks. When the farmer puts them all together, how many haystacks will he have?

3. From five feet high,
   Up to the sky,
   It reaches, though 'tis round;
   Now try your wits, if fancy hits,
   This riddle you'll expound.

4. This question is from 'A Tangled Tale' by Lewis Carroll, and there are two possible answers. (If not more.)
   Bill and Ben began the year with £1,000 each. They borrowed nothing, they stole nothing, they inherited nothing, they earned nothing, they won nothing, they were given nothing – and yet – by the next New Year's day they had many millions between them.
   How did they do it? (And I reckon that's a question worth answering.)

Answers: Number 3 at the end of the book.

And now – think of yourself (that's U) – double it (that's W) – add nought (that's WO) – add a small number (that's No.) – take away nought (that's N) – and the answer's: WON!

Charades

This isn't actually the game when you act out the syllables but the idea's the same. All you do is split up a word into its syllables, and describe them one at a time, sometimes putting the whole word at the end, as well. (Which usually gives the game away.)

They were always a popular kind of riddle – in Jane Austen's day and long before that. Try these.

1. My first makes company.
   My second shuns company.
   My third assembles company.
   My whole puzzles company.

2. My first I hope you are.
   My second I see you are.
   My whole I know you are.

3. My first is snapping, snarling, growling.
   My second's industrious, romping, and prowling.

Answers: 1. *Conundrum*   2. *Welcome*   3. *Currants*

✳

LOOK AT HIM THERE, ACTING THE FOOL

WHAT MAKES YOU THINK HE'S ACTING?

Rules of the Society

1. No *robin'* is allowed – while they cannot belong, a short while is alright.

2. No member may ask a *chicken* why it is crossing the road – it either has its own *fowl* reasons, or it's trying to commit suicide. 3. There's a duty on *petrels*.

4. No member may *crow* over, or *rail*, or *'owl*, or *snipe* at another, but once *bittern* they are expected not to *grouse*.

5. Take your *tern* nicely, but please remember to return him later, because one good *tern* deserves another. 6. *Jay*-walkers will find themselves up before the beak, and may be fined, when found, of course (and fined double if found off course).

7. Anyone up to *larks* will have *swift* punishment. 8. *Cranes* are useful and can have a year's free membership – also *yellow-hammers*.

9. *Blackbirds* are welcome. 10. If any member is *cuckoo* enough to start *raven'* he can go fly a *kite*.

11. If one member *swallows* another, that's not summer, that's cannibalism. 12. All birds are expected to be female.

13. *Toucan* join for the price of one. 14. *Vultures* are requested not to use the canteen, but to eat the car cases in the car parks. 15. The *chiff-chaff* can join with rest of the riff-raff.

16. *Hawks and doves* are asked not to talk politics on the premises, as it makes the feathers fly.

Branches all over the country

Somethin's Brewing!

Written after looking up Q in the dictionary.

The wood
Of the quassia tree
In the form of chips
Is made into medicine
(And sometimes into ships).

If boiled
With soap and water
You will find it quite the thing
For catching caterpillars
On a currant bush in spring.

If you're faint
Or quaint, or queezy;
If you think you've got the plague,
Just quaffa
Cup of quassia
Very quickly,
From a quaigh.

Oh, its bark is very bitter,
And its bite just like a sting;
But the quassia, without question,
Is a quintessential thing.

Cautionary Tales

A KILLING JOKE

His young son Jim
Would tell his pa
Such funny jokes,
He laughed, ha-ha.

But then one day
Jim heard a clonk,
Pa'd laughed his head off,
Ha-ha bonk.

So please take care;
Your funny joke
May be the death
Of some poor bloke.

RESTLESS JANE

Young Jane
Was always on the go,
And guzzling food
While to and fro.

She gobbled toast
And cakes and buns
While executing
Skips and runs.

She danced around
And sang a tune
And drank her tea
And then – the spoon.

Oh poor young Jane,
How sad for her –
For now alas
She CANNOT STIR!

ACID HUMOUR

Poor old Brown is dead and gone
His face you'll see no more,
For what he thought was H_2O
Was H_2SO_4.

Died on Wednesday

This tombstone actually comes from a place called Tombstone, in Arizona. It was put up to commemorate a man called Lester Moore, a Wells Fargo agent, who was shot in a dispute.

HERE
LIES
LESTER MOORE
FOUR SLUGS
FROM A44
NO LES
NO MORE

Cannibal Customs

What do cannibals play at parties?

> Swallow my leader.

> Cannibal husband: 'How many people for dinner tonight, darling?'

> Cannibal wife: 'Just one each, dear.'

What did the cannibal say when he was late for dinner?

> 'I say, has everyone been eaten already?'

> Cannibal husband: 'What's for lunch, dear?'
> Cannibal wife: 'Just soup and a sandwich-man.'
> Cannibal husband: 'Can't you open a tin of someone?'

If a boy ate his father and mother, what would that make him?

> An orphan.

> Cannibal: 'How much do you charge for dinner here?'
> Waiter: '£2 a head, sir.'
> Cannibal: 'Well, I'll have a couple of legs too, please.'

> Cannibal: 'Waiter, what kind of beans are these?'

> Waiter: 'Human beans, sir.'

Why should you always keep calm when you meet cannibals?

> Because you don't want to get in a stew, do you?

THE CANNIBAL BIRD

The cannibal bird
Can never be seen,
It can only be heard.

And it feeds on high ground,
And pigmy stew,
So I'd keep out of sound –
If I were you.

USEFUL INVENTIONS OF DAYS GONE BY

With Kumfyride

Without Kumfyride

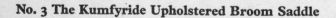

Extra pillion seats suitable for cats, toads, etc.

No. 3 The Kumfyride Upholstered Broom Saddle

Things Ain't What They Seem

TOPSY-TURVY THINGS

What come at night, without being fetched, and are lost in the day, without being stolen?

The stars.

What goes all through the house but never touches a thing?

A voice.

What went to the North Pole and stopped there, and came back because it wouldn't go there?

A watch.

What goes round the wood, but can never get into the wood?

The bark.

What can pass in front of the sun without making a shadow?

The wind.

What is greater than God; worse than the Devil; the dead eat it: if you eat it, you'll die?

Nothing.

There was a man who sat up all night wondering where on earth the sun had gone to.

Next morning it dawned on him.

One fine day in the middle of the night
Two dead men got up to fight.
Back to back they faced each other,
Drew their swords and shot each other.
A paralysed donkey passing by
Kicked a blind man in the eye,
Knocked him through a rubber wall
Into a dry ditch and drowned them all.

King Rabssaldschal and the Clever Wife

This is a Tibetan tale. The story goes that King Rabssald-schal was on bad terms with a neighbouring king. This king wanted to test how keen-witted and sharp King Rabssaldschal's first minister was, before letting matters go from bad to worse and making war on King Rab. So he posed three problems for the minister to answer.

Luckily the minister had a very sharp-witted and clever wife, who was able to advise him.

First of all, the king sent to King Rabssaldschal two mares. They were dam and filly, mother and daughter, and identical. Would King Rabssaldschal say which was which? King Rabssaldschal sent for his minister, and his minister sent for his wife.

'Put some grass in front of them,' she said. 'The mother will push the best grass towards the foal.' And it was so. King Rabssaldschal (with the help of the minister's wife), gave the correct answer.

Next the king sent two snakes. Again, they looked identical. 'Which is the male and which the female?' asked the king.

'Put them on cotton-wool,' said the minister's wife. 'The female will lie quiet, but the male will not. Females like things soft and comfortable, but males can't bear it.' And again she was right.

Finally the king sent just one long stick of wood. It was of equal thickness along the whole of its length, there were no knots, and no marks at all on it. 'Which is the upper, and which the lower end?' asked the king. It seemed impossible. King Rabssaldschal hadn't the faintest idea, nor his minister. But the minister's wife said:

'Put the stick in water. The root end will sink a little, and the upper end will float.' So they did. And she was right. The end nearer the root was just a little bit heavier, and dipped in the water.

The minister gave his answer, and the neighbouring king was confounded by his cleverness.

(*I don't know what happened then, but I suppose he thought he had better tread a little warily with King Rabssaldschal, who had such a brilliant minister at his command.*)

This is only one story of a great number which are known by the description, 'The Clever Lass', stories where a clever woman either solves very difficult riddles, or makes up some herself, and generally runs rings round the man in question.

Doctor, I keep thinking I'm a bridge.
What's come over you, man?
Four cars, two lorries and five buses.

Mick and Mulligan
on Wednesday

MICK: Which would you say was better, Mulligan, complete happiness or a cheese sandwich?
MULLIGAN: I'd say complete happiness, Mick.
MICK: And you'd be wrong, boyo. A cheese sandwich is better, 'cos nothing is better than complete happiness, and a cheese sandwich is better than nothing.
MULLIGAN: And that's logical, Mick, so it is.

MICK: There's the devil of a lot of traffic, Mulligan, and me trying to cross the road.
MULLIGAN: There's a zebra crossing down there, Mick.
MICK: Sure, and I hope he has more luck than me.

MICK: What are you doing walking about the streets with that bread and butter?

MULLIGAN: Looking for the traffic jam, Mick.

MICK: Why don't you go for a tramp in the woods with the dog, then?

MULLIGAN: Ah to be sure, but the tramp was getting in such a devil of a temper.

*

Read It Aloud!

There was once a headmaster of Winchester, who used to make every boy read this out, to see if he could put the emphasis on the right words. Try it!

I saw that C saw.
C saw that that I saw.
I saw that that that C saw was so.
C saw that, that that that I saw was so.
I saw that, that that, that that C saw was so.
C saw that that that, that that that that I saw was so.
I saw that that, that that that that C saw was so.

(The clue is to remember that the 'that' in the first line stands for 'that thing which' – or does that make it worse?)

Mother: 'Please keep quiet, Tom. Your father's trying to read.'

Tom: 'Crikey, I learnt how to do that *years* ago.'

The Leith police dismisseth us,
  I'm thankful, sir, to say;
The Leith police dismisseth us,
  They thought we sought to stay.
The Leith police dismisseth us,
  We both sighed sighs apiece,
And the sigh that we sighed as we said good-bye
  Was the size of the Leith police.

The rehearsal was due to begin at 11.00 a.m. At 12.00 a.m. the Loyal Sympathy Orchestra was Less Loyal and Pretty Unsympathetic. At 12.30 a.m. the air was electric on account of the guitars being wrongly plugged in and the orchestra was Completely Unloyal and Quite Pathetic. At 12.31 Sir Phil Harmonic entered the Hall.

He smoothed the crease in his pin-stripes, tossed his hair back, saying 'Thank you very much' to the second violin, who returned it, and tapped his bat on the podium. Whereupon someone shouted: 'How's that?'

'Not out,' replied Sir Phil, and they had two minute's silence in sympathy for the music they were about to play. Then the whole orchestra ran through the Air on a G-string, which made them shiver.

'And now,' announced Sir Phil gravely, 'We will take the last movement of Shoeman's Carnival of Animals – the Zebra Crossing.' The orchestra went smartly through that until finally it died gracefully away, to the sound of the last haunting melody sung by the Bark Choir.

The Orchestra next attempted to play Mozart's Wolfgang Overture. Unfortunately the wolf gang got out of hand from the start. They tore the music to shreds, and raced through the cellos. Sir Phil lost his cool and then his trousers, as the wolves, howling for food, ate the cornets and then started on the trombones.

Soon the whole Hall was in uproar. The violins put their strings to their bows and aimed. 'Oboes, Oboes.' shouted Sir Phil despairingly, clutching at his ankles. 'Where's the glockenspiel?'

The noise rose to a tremendous crescendo. Cymbals clashed into French horns. Paper, drums, woodwind, every kind of instrument was flung into the air as the wolves made for the door.

Sir Phil defiantly held his trousers with his left hand and raised his baton with his right for the grand finale. The sound was so deafening that it raised the roof, leaving the entire orchestra open to the sky.

Finally, it was the rain that stopped play.

As the Witch said to the Skeleton

WITCH: 'Come on out of that cupboard.'
SKELETON: 'I can't. I haven't got the face to.'

WITCH: 'Oh, come on. There's a dance down the road. Why don't you go?'
SKELETON: 'I haven't any body to go with.'

WITCH: 'Don't you know *anyone*?'
SKELETON: 'No, I haven't got a single ghoul-friend.'

WITCH: 'Well, you needn't sound so sorry for yourself.'
SKELETON: 'Well, I've lost my voice, among other things I haven't got a leg to stand on.'

WITCH: 'I suppose you were trying to throw yourself off that cliff yesterday ?'
SKELETON: 'No, I hadn't got the guts.'

WITCH: 'Scared, eh ?'
SKELETON: 'Me scared ? You couldn't make *me* jump out of my skin, if you tried.'

WITCH: 'I don't know why I bother with you – you're just a bone-idle old bonehead.'
SKELETON: 'That's right.'

Wednesday's Shaggy Dog Story

It was a dark and stormy Wednesday night. The wind was howling in the trees as Ben & Bob staggered home from the pub, and along the winding lanes. As they came past the churchyard, they saw a sack lying in the road.

They looked inside, and found it was full of peanuts. Bob said they ought to take it to the police. But Ben said: 'No, don't let's bother with that. Let's share them out.' 'Alright,' agreed Bob, 'but it's got to be fair, mind.' Ben picked up the sack, to go into the churchyard, but dropped a couple of peanuts by the churchyard gate. 'Hey, you've dropped two,' said Bob. 'We'll come back for those later,' said Ben, and they went in and sat on a gravestone, to count out the peanuts. By the light of a torch they sat in the howling gale, on the gravestone, and shared them out.

A little while later a small boy was coming home along the lane. He'd just been to see *The Blood-red Vampire* at the cinema, and his head was whirling with vampires and dead bodies. And as he came near the churchyard he saw a weird light and heard voices saying, 'One for you, and one for me. One for you, and one for me.'

The boy turned and fled. He found a policeman and panted out 'There are two devils in the churchyard, counting out the dead bodies.' The policeman pooh-poohed the whole idea. 'There's no such thing,' he said. But he agreed to come along and have a look.

Back to the churchyard gate they went, in the dark and the howling wind. And by the time they got there, the men had finished counting. Just as they got outside the gate, they saw the light flickering, and the dark shapes of the yew trees, and the dim shadows of the gravestones, and they heard a voice say:

'AND DON'T FORGET THE TWO OUT-SIDE THE GATE.'

And they *both* ran.

Why are children told not to whisper?
Because it's not aloud.

Thursday's Horoscope

Do you want to double your money today? Then don't waste time. Fold it at once.

Avoid the countryside today. It could be dangerous. The flowers have pistils. And if you don't want to be burnt, then wear a coat, not a blazer.

Someone will write you a letter today (U) – and you'll make lots of new friends. I can see a large dark person, with a big mouth and covered with flowers. That's a hippy-potamus. The stars also reveal something that's alive and has only one foot. It could be your leg.

Finally, a warning to Eskimos: Don't give a house-warming party today.

And when you go to bed, take a ruler with you – to see how long you sleep.

LOTS OF SCOPE FOR HORROR ON THURSDAY

*

And I expect you'd like to hear the one about the bed? Sorry, but it hasn't been made yet.

What the Fortune-Teller Told

Bill Smith went to a fortune-teller one day, who said, 'I won't *tell* you your fortune, because I don't want to frighten you, but I'll write it down and put it in this locket.' So the fortune-teller put Bill Smith's fortune in the locket, and made him swear never to look at it, until his dying day.

Some time later, Bill joined the Army. On his first night in camp, the man next to him said 'I say, let's have a look in that locket,' and before Bill could stop him, he had. The effect was extraordinary. In no time at all Bill was called before the C.O., who said, 'I'm sorry Smith, but we can't have chaps like you in the army. We'll have to chuck you out.' Which they did.

So Bill Smith enlisted in the Navy. And his very first night in uniform, someone said, 'I say, let's have a look in that locket,' and they had a look inside. And in no time at all, Bill Smith was called before the Admiral. 'I'm sorry, Smith,' he said, 'but we can't have chaps like you in the Navy. We'll have to chuck you out.' Which they did.

So Bill Smith thought he'd try the Air-force. He signed up, and very soon found himself in camp. The first night, as he was undressing, he looked nervously at the man nearest to him, but he had noticed nothing. Nor the next night, nor the one after that. 'So that's alright,' thought Bill. 'Thank goodness. At least I shall be able to stay in the Air-force.'

He was on his first flight over the sea, when the fellow next to him, leant over and said, 'I say, that's a very fine locket. Mind if I have a look inside?' And before Bill could do anything about it, he had.

And in no time at all, the Wing-Commander was standing over him. 'I'm sorry, Smith,' he said, 'but we can't have chaps like you in the Air-force; we'll have to chuck you out.' Which they did. But as they were about 20,000 feet up, they gave him a parachute, and an inflatable raft.

Bill Smith drifted over the sea on his raft, until he reached a tiny desert island. He sat on the sand, and thought, 'Well, this must be my dying day,' so he opened the locket, and got the piece of paper out, with his fortune written on it, and was just about to read it, when the wind came and blew it out to sea . . .

Calling All Aquarians!

GETTING WET ON THURSDAY

There was an old man and his daughter
Who fell head over heels in deep water.
    Said the man, 'Her can't swim,'
    (And no more couldn't him)
'I wish someone had tortoise, or taughter.'

Another hopeless washout.

ANYONE FOR A DIP?

What goes into the water red and comes out black?
  A red hot poker.

What goes into the water black and comes out red?
  A lobster.

What goes into the water red and can't be red any more?
  A book.

What goes into the water white and comes out black?
  A miller's boot.

What goes into the water pink and comes out blue?
  A swimmer on a cold day.

What goes into the water white and comes out brown?
  A cow on a snowy day.

*

AQUARIUS says: How can you carry water in a sieve?
When it's frozen.

Riddles of History Answered

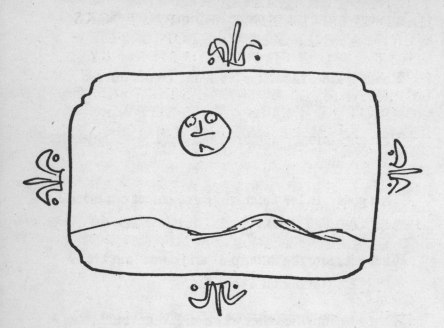

What did the man in the moon think of the man on the moon?

The following message was transmitted from the moon via satellite. It slipped through the tracking stations at both Jodrell Bank and the Houston Space Centre – but was finally received by a radio ham sandwich in Leamington Spa. (Yet another triumph for Britain's amateur radio caterers.)

We apologize for a certain amount of interference. The ham sandwich was half-eaten and lying in the road at the time. However, it was picked up by Andrew Cunningham, of 24a Upper Station Villas, who also picked off the gravel, and decoded it. The notes are his.

DEAR NEIL ARMSTRONG MANY
THANKS FOR DELIVERING THE
HARDWARE ON TIME STOP STOCKS
WERE RUNNING LOW STOP BUT
WHAT ON EARTH DO YOU MEAN BY
ONE SMALL STEP? STOP IT ALL
DEPENDS WHO YOU ARE STEPPING ON
DOESN'T IT? STOP YOU GOT ME
RIGHT IN THE LUMBAR* REGIONS
STOP NEXT TIME DON'T BOTHER
DELIVERING THE STUFF STOP JUST
SEND IT STOP I NEED A NEW CAR
STOP AND WOULD YOU GIVE A
MESSAGE TO THOSE OTHER GREAT
BIG FLATFOOTED . . . . . † OF YOURS?
STOP STOP STOP SIGNED . . . . . ‡

* lunar?
† missing section missing due to being trodden on
‡ signature eaten

This historic message is now on display at the Science
Museum, South Kensington, London – under glass. To
keep the air out, and the pong in.

Those wishing to view had better hurry.

Died on Thursday

The outward case
Of William Chase
(Maker of clocks)
Lies in this box.

His life wound up,
His time done here,
Dear Maker, please
This one repair

And set him going,
Clean and mended
Till Time itself
One day is ended.

Who Said . . . ?

'Why don't you drop in sometime?'
   The puddle to the rain.

'Fancy running into you like this.'
   The river to the sea.

'Will you join me?'
   One handcuff to the other.

'Darling, you're a perfect worm!'
   The earthworm to his fiancée.

'I wish I felt on top of the world.'
   Atlas – to himself.

'Now son, don't get into a jam.'
   Mother strawberry to baby strawberry.

'Hello, sucker.'
   The lollipop to the boy.

And what did the scissors say to the paper?
I'm not sure, but I know it was some cutting remark.

ARIES: *The Ram*

No. 4 Sibthorpe's Suction Footwear

Essential for the Young Person: with Sibthorpe's
superior suckers you carry on music practice, home-
work, stamp-collecting, etc., without interference from
your brothers and sisters.

Food on Thursday

MAN: 'Hey, waiter. There's a spider in my lettuce.'
WAITER: 'Yes, sir. I didn't know you were a vegetarian.'

MAN: 'Tell me, waiter, who's that terribly ill-looking
man over there ?'
WAITER: 'Our oldest customer, sir.'

MAN: 'Waiter, can we have another candle at our table,
please ?'
WAITER: 'Certainly sir. With cream ?'

MAN: 'Hey waiter, what's this fly doing in my soup ?'
WAITER: 'The crawl, I think, sir.'

MAN: 'I'll have apple-pie without custard, please.'
WAITER: 'Sorry sir, we don't serve it with custard. You'll
have to have it without cream.'

MAN: 'Waiter, this steak is undercooked. It's absolutely bloody.'
WAITER: 'Well, what do you expect in a ruddy awful
restaurant like this ?'

*

I HEAR YOU'VE TAKEN UP FOOTBALL

I'M ONLY DOING IT FOR THE KICKS

An Eskimo went into a restaurant one day, with a seal and a polar bear. He called to the head waiter and said: 'Waiter, do you serve oysters in this restaurant?' The waiter said: 'Certainly sir, we always serve oysters first.' So the Eskimo ordered a table for four, and taking an oyster out of his pocket, said to it, 'That's alright, you sit next to me, and they'll serve you first.'

PISCES: the fishes. What happened when there was a fight in the fish shop?
Two fish got battered. So watch out today.

SOUNDS DELISHES

Limericks

CALLING ALL DRS!

When you think of the hosts without No.,
Who are slain by the deadly cuco.,
   It's quite a mistake
   Of such food to partake,
It results in a permanent slo.

PCRUMBS!

There was a young lady called Psyche,
Who was heard to ejaculate, 'Pcryche!'
   For when riding her pbych,
   She ran into a ptrych,
And fell on some rails that were pspyche.

There was a young lady called Maud,
Who was the most terrible fraud.
   To eat, when at table,
   She never was able,
But when in the larder – oh, Gawd!

There was a young man of Herne Bay,
Who was making some fireworks one day;
    But he dropped his cigar
    In the gunpowder jar . . .
There *was* a young man of Herne Bay!

GOLD'N FEATHERS

Only one of these answers is a catch. The other two are perfectly genuine!

1. Which is heavier, a pound of gold, or a pound of feathers?
    A. A pound of feathers.
2. Which weighs more, an ounce of gold, or an ounce of feathers?
    A. An ounce of gold.
3. Which is the greater weight, one bar of gold, or one feather?
    A. One feather.

If you're curious to know which *and* why – *see Answer Number 4 at the end of the book.*

CANCER: the crab. A boy put his foot in the water, and said 'Ouch.' What was that? A splash and crab raid.

There used to be something of a craze for epigrams, especially in the 17th century. They are very close to riddles –
only the question and answer are folded in together.
These are some poets' epigrams.

I am unable, yonder beggar cries,
To stand or move; if he say true, he lies.
(John Donne, 1572–1631)
Treason doth never prosper; what's the reason?
For if it prosper, none dare call it treason.
(printed 1618, anon.)

'Twixt kings and tyrants there's this difference known,
Kings seek their subjects' good; tyrants their own.

(Robert Herrick, 1591–1674)

One asked a madman if a wife he had.
A wife? quoth he – I never was so mad.

(Robert Hayman, published 1628)

Mick and Mulligan

MICK: What's the safest colour to wear in the streets
at night, Mulligan?

MULLIGAN: Is it white, then, so the cars can see you?

MICK: Sure, and that's what O'Grady thought. He dressed all in white, O'Grady did – his shirt. his tie, his trousers – everything was white, And then he was run down by a snow-plough

MICK: Mulligan, do you know why a fire engine is red?

MULLIGAN: Not really, no.

MICK: Well, it's because it has eight men and four wheels: four plus eight is equal to the sum of twelve; twelve inches make a ruler; one of the best rulers was Queen Elizabeth, who ruled over the Seven Seas; in the Seven Seas are fish; fish have fins; the Finns fought the Russians, and the Russian flag is red.

MULLIGAN: And that's logical, so it is.

MICK: I saw this man in the train the other day, Mulligan. He had a great big jar of salt, and a great big pile of bananas. And all the time he kept opening this jar of salt, dipping a banana into it, and then what do you think he did?

MULLIGAN: He ate it?

MICK: Not at all – not at all Mulligan. Now this fellow wasn't stupid – he didn't like salt on bananas, so he threw them out of the window.

LEO: the lion. A Christian was thrown into the arena with a lion, and fell down on his knees to pray. Then he saw the lion praying too. And the lion said: 'I don't know what you're saying, but I'm saying grace.'

Missing – on Thursday
NOTICE

A plain gold (twenty-two-carat) ring disappeared
from the changing-room at the Golf
Club on Thursday afternoon.

Police wish to interview any
Donkey who is engaged, but can't spell.

*

*Gemini! The Twins. If I saw you standing by a
monkey, what fruit
would I think of?
A Pear.*

THE RIDDLE OF THE
IVORY WALKING-STICKS

There was a robbery down at the Witsend Museum the other day. When the news came in to Witsend Police Station, Sergeant Duffer happened to be on duty. 'What's all this then?' he said. 'Three Indian ivory canes stolen? Very valuable. Hand-carved with monkeys and elephants? H'm. I'd better go down and have a look.'

So he did. The Museum Director was completely mystified.

'The ivory canes were in this glass case,' he said. 'But the glass isn't broken. Nothing's broken. There's not a window smashed in the place, and the doors are still locked. I can't think how the blighter got in – or got out. The thing's impossible.'

'H'm,' said Sergeant Duffer to himself, and had a quick dekko around the place.

'Hello, hello, hello,' he said at last. 'Here's three small holes in the wooden frame of the case. And here's three more, right at the bottom of the wall. H'm.' (Sergeant Duffer was well-known for his humming.) 'Now that's very significacious. An inside job, I'd say.'

And right away, he knew who to look for. Who was it?

Answer: Number 5 at the end of the book.

This is an anagram: These look like MOON-STARERS.
Answer: ASTRONOMERS!

Taurus
ALL I KNOW ABOUT BULLS

What I know about bulls
Is really risible,*
Cos I always take care
That I'm here

and

the

bull

is

so

far

away

it

is

hardly

visible.

*laughable
(which bulls aren't)

hardly visi-bull.

The Thutton Typewriter Thervice,
12 New Thtreet,
Thutton, Thurrey

Dear Thir,
   Will you pleathe thend thomeone to mend thith typewriter. Thith ith the thecond one we have had from you
on which the eth key doeth not work.

                    Yorth thincerely,
                    T. Thamuelth

Mr T. Zamuelz

Dear Zir,
   We quite underztand your trouble, and will be zending
zomeone round az zoon az pozzible.

                    Yourz zincerely,
                    The Zutton Typewriter Zervice

                    *

I think I must be SCORPIO because I've got a sting in my tail, too.

Un-humdrum Conundrums

Can February march?

  No. But April may.

If April showers bring May flowers, what do May flowers bring?

  Pilgrims.

What's brown and wrinkled and glowing?

  An electric prune.

What's the difference between a hill and a pill?

  One is hard to get up, and the other is hard to get down.

What is copper nitrate?

  Overtime for policemen.

How does a sparrow with engine trouble manage to land safely?

  With it's sparrow chute.

There were three tomatoes in the desert. Which one was the cowboy?

  None of them. They were all redskins.

If crocodiles make good shoes, what do banana skins make?

  Good slippers.

What goes from branch to branch, and wears a bowler hat?

A bank manager.

If you had two wires, and you took one away, what would you have?

A wireless.

What's a tin of corned beef?

An armoured cow.

Why do bees hum?

Because they don't know the words.

What's worse than an Indian on the warpath?

A banana skin on the footpath.

What was the first smoke-signal sent by an Indian?

Help! My blanket is on fire!

✳

SAGITTARIUS: the archer. Take your bow into the woods with you today – the buds could be shooting.

I keep getting these shooting pains in my back.

Real Puzzlers – 1

(Only people with real *brains should have a go at these – sawdust and cotton wool will get you nowhere, sorry.)*

1. What question must you *always* answer YES to?

2. What question can you *never* answer Yes to – *even though it's true?*

3. If a group of people contain:
   a father, mother, uncle, aunt, sister, brother, nephew, niece, and two cousins,
   what is the *smallest number* of people they can be?

4. What is it that occurs four times in every week; twice in every month; and only once in a year?

5. A man wants to carry three things across a river – a fox, a chicken, and a sack of wheat.
   The only trouble is that he cannot at any time leave the

*

LIBRA: the scales. What does the QE2 weigh when it leaves Southampton? It's anchor.

chicken with the wheat, or he'll eat it – or the fox with the chicken, or *he'll* eat *it*! *And* he can only take one thing with him in his boat at one time.
How does he get them across?

6. Now, imagine there is a large live duck inside a very large bottle. The bottle is made of glass, and has a very narrow neck.
How can you get the duck out of the bottle, without breaking it, or hurting the duck?

Before you go round the bend – the answers are Number 6 at the end of the book.

Jest Animals

How do you get four elephants into a Mini?
>   Two in the back and two in the front.

And how do you get two whales in a car?
>   Along the M4 and across the Severn Bridge.

What's small and feathery and goes phut-phut-phut?
>   An outboard budgie.

What do baby apes sleep in?
>   Apricots.

What did the pony say when he coughed?
>   'Excuse me, I'm just a little hoarse.'

Where do tadpoles go to change into frogs?
>   The croakroom.

Why is a pig the strangest animal in the farmyard?
>   Because first he's killed, and then he's cured.

Why does a giraffe eat very little?
>   Because he makes a little go a long way.

When is a yellow dog most likely to come into your house?
>   When the door's open.

Why were the bees on strike?
>   Shorter flowers and more honey.

How do you catch a monkey?

> Hang upside down in a tree and make a noise like a banana.

What are the little white things in your head that bite?

> Teeth.

Why did the tortoise beat the hare?

> There's nothing faster than Shell.

✳

CAPRICORN: the goat. When is a goat nearly? When it's all butt.

Jography

Monsieur Porcupine swept into the room as usual, handed the broom over to one of the boys to get on with it, aimed his pile of exercise books at the desk, missed, fell over the broom, picked himself up, rubbing out what was on the blackboard at the same time, said 'Good Morning, boys,' and rubbed his hands with pleasure, forgetting they were covered with grease from his left-hand-drive bike.

'Good morning, Monsieur Porcupine.'

'Why's he looking so pleased with himself this morning?'

'Zees morning, boys, I 'ave got a leetle test for you. On ze Belle France, and ze Common Market, and ze eekonomics. Plis to get your pens ready.'

'You will see zat zair ees a leetle box after each question. Please to put ze right answer in it.'

So everyone got down to the test.

1. A woman who works in a sweet shop in Copenhagen is 5 ft 2 ins tall, measures 42-33-46, and takes size 10 shoes. What does she weigh?
   (a) 16 stones   (b) sweets   ☐

2. Why would you be crazy to bathe in the river in Paris?

    (a) You'd be arrested (b) You'd be in Seine ☐

3. If a ton of coal costs £14 in Aberdeen, what does a load of firewood come to in Aachen?

    (a) 150 francs (b) ashes (c) the front door ☐

4. How many girls would it take to reach from London to Aberdeen? (A miss is as good as a mile.)

    (a) 793 (b) 492 (c) 1,983 ☐

5. If tomatoes are 15p a lb. in Manchester, what are window-panes in Brussels?

    (a) 1,760 pfennigs (b) glass
    (c) glass and 1,760 pfennigs ☐

Everyone did the test easily, and then someone asked what to do with the boxes.

'Pile zem in the corner,' said Monsieur Porcupine.

'But are they going to be marked?'

'Don't vorry,' said Monsieur Porcupine, airily. 'Zey will be marked, franced, pounded, made into old krones, guilded, French polished, sent by registered post, exported, imported, re-exported, re-imported, and returned for you in plenty of time for ze Jewish New Year.'

*

VIRGO: There's one of those lovely girls from Harmondsworth come to see us.

A pretty young teacher named Beauchamp,
Said, 'These awful boys, how shall I teauchamp?
  For they will not behave,
  Although I look grave,
And with tears in my eyes I beseauchamp.'

There was an old woman who lived in a shoe,
And had so many children she didn't know what to do.
But when they grew up, and she'd no one to handle,
The old woman moved out, and into a sandal!

The Earth and Space
on Thursday

What holds the sun up in the sky?
  The sunbeams.

How do we know the earth will never come to an end?
  Because it is round.

Why doesn't the sea spill over the earth?
  Because it is tide.

What did one Martian say to the other, as they came near
Earth?
  'You'll like this place, it has atmosphere!'

What do you call a spaceman's watch?
  A lunartick.

And why isn't Monaco sending a rocket to the moon this year?

They can't find a bottle big enough to hold the stick.

Once upon a time a guide was explaining things to a group of tourists.

'These rocks,' he said, 'were piled up by the glaciers.'

'But where are the glaciers?' asked Mrs Nuttybun.

'They've gone back, madam,' replied the guide, 'to get some more rocks.'

Where do you find giant snails?

On a giant's fingers.

*

Where does **PA'S NANNY LIVE** in America?

ΡΕΝΝSΥLVΑΝΙΑ

— *Well what about A FRANTIC SNIFF UP EAST?*

— *Don't be ridiculous. Everyone knows PUFFINS ARE FANTASTIC.*

SO WHAT'S ON THE MENU FOR

FRIDAY?

FROM WHAT I'VE SEEN, IT'S MOSTLY CHESTNUTS.

The sausage is a cunning bird,
With feathers long and wavy;
It swims about the frying pan
And makes its nest in gravy.

Trifle

(I must explain first of all that the Stuffins have been holding a meeting of their Cookery Club, in the Village Hall. Four Stuffins, and the Chairman, have stayed behind. I can't really explain what a Stuffin looks like, except that they have rather long noses, and curly hair.)

'Why, my dear fellows,' said the Chairman, 'how good to see you again. Just in time, just in time, for the best part of the meeting – the eating.' And he shepherded them up to the platform, and busied himself laying the table, and then picking it up again.

'Take a pew, take a pew,' he said grandly. Sam Stuffin took some time over this, as they were bolted to the floor.

Soon everyone was seated. Delicious smells were coming

from one side of the platform. The Chairman had vanished. Oniony, beany, bacony, friedy chipsy smells wafted over the table. There was a tremendous sound of battering. Then smoke slithered round the door of what had been clearly, but was now dimly, the kitchen.

Soon, the table was enveloped in a thick cloud. It was Uncle Stuffin who cut them out of it, with his knife and fork. And at the same moment, the door burst open, and the Chairman came through, beaming as ever, carrying the most beaten-up old pot you've ever seen. (Or ever will.)

'I've made a tremendous hash of everything,' he announced triumphantly. 'But I've knocked up something that you will never forget. A trifle *bien cuite*, as the French say, but no *mere* trifle. This' – (with a great flourish of napkins) – 'This – is the most exceptional trifle I have ever trifled with.'

The Stuffins looked eager. They were hungry. Everyone tucked in with knife and fork and gusto.

What was it like?

Of those who ate that trifle, only one now survives. As far as he can remember it contained: about enough chips for 17 people; 2 pints of cream; a tin of sliced peaches; 22 bacon rashers (crisp); 14 lamb cutlets; several pounds of strawberries; a dot of curry powder and a dash of pepper; several sponge cakes (crumbled); a couple of dozen eggs (coddled); 3 pints of mayonnaise; 2 portions of fried fish; 11 tins of baked beans; the whole thing topped with custard – and meringues floating delicately on the top.

The Chairman was so pleased with this dish that he promised to cook it again at the next meeting of the Club. Uncle Stuffin, who told me this story, said he always happened to be rather busy after that on Cookery Club nights, so he didn't know if it went down well – or if it went down at all, come to that.

A gentleman, dining at Crewe,
Found quite a large mouse in his stew.
  Said the waiter, 'Don't shout,
  And wave it about,
Or the rest will be wanting one, too!'

MAN: 'Waiter, this boiled egg is as hard as a rock.'

WAITER: 'I can't think why, sir. It's been cooking all morning.'

MAN: 'Hey, waiter, there's a small beetle in this cabbage.'

WAITER: 'Sorry sir. Shall I get you a bigger one?'

MAN: 'Hey, waiter, what's this animal doing, singing hymns on my plate?'

WAITER: 'It's a Welsh rabbit, sir.'

MAN: 'Waiter, I don't like the look of these chips. They're all red, white, and blue.'

WAITER: 'That's right, sir. French fried potatoes.'

MAN: 'Hey waiter, this dinner was a disgrace. In fact, I doubt if you could serve me a more disgusting, filthy, and revolting meal if you tried.'

WAITER: 'Oh, I don't know sir. Why don't you come again tomorrow, and I'll see what I can do?'

Limericks on Friday

Here lies a fat gluttonous sinner.
(Now he's dead he's considerably thinner.)
He's gone, so they tell,
Without doubt to – well –
To the place where they cook a hot dinner.

Two greedy young boys from Streatham
Bought fifty-five doughnuts – and eatham.
The coroner said,
'No wonder they're dead,
How unwise of their parents to leatham.'

Long legged Italy
Kicked poor Sicily
Right in the middle of the Mediterranean Sea.
Austria was Hungary,
Took a bit of Turkey,
Dipped it in Greece,
Fried it in Japan,
And ate it off China.

Hey, wait a minute – there's a better way of serving Turkey than that.
How?
Join the Turkish army.

Read it Aloud!

This is positively one of the worst tongue-twisters I know.
(To be repeated six times after every meal.)
Swan swam over the sea,
Swim, swan, swim.
Swan swam back again,
Well swum swan.

*

When is a Scotsman like a donkey?
When he strolls along his banks and braes.

Died on Friday

Is it Latin? Or Dutch? Or double Dutch?

```
        BENE
    A·T·H  T·H  I·S·S·T
    ONELI   ET   HEM
   O·R·T  AL  REMA·I·N
       SOF  B  ILLE
          VAN
       SA  ND  HI
      S·Y  O·U  N
       GD  AUGH
        T·E·R·K
         A·T·E
```

*

(KATE.)
HIS YOUNG DAUGHTER
AND
OF BILL EVANS
LIE THE MORTAL REMAINS
BENEATH THIS STONE
(Don't worry – it's English.

The Fisherman's Story

There was once a fisherman who went out fishing and the only fish he caught was so tiny, he threw it away. But he went into a pub on the way home, and told a story about the fish he *nearly* caught.

He said it was as big as this:

And then he had another drink,
and said it was as big as this:

And then he had another
drink,
and said it was as big as this:

And then he stumbled home
across the fields in the
moonlight,
and saw this:

And the fisherman exclaimed: 'My dear chap, you've really gone too far this time.'

THIS IS A DROODLE

What is it?

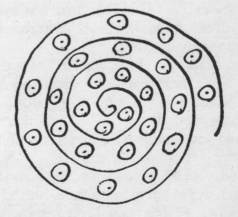

Lots of Mexicans going
up a hill.

Fry Day's Dinner:
Can You Spell? Part Two

Remember Part One? How the witch was just about to put Tom into the calldron? 'What's next,' he asked. 'Then it's U,' she said . . . Now read on . . .

'Oh, I shouldn't put yew in. It's poisonous,' said Tom.

'Not yew, you, U,' screamed the witch, almost beside herself with rage, but she just managed to keep in one piece. And she was just getting her skinny fingers on Tom's jacket, when he ducked.

'Now,' he said, very carefully, from the other side of the calldron. 'Calm down, Mum. I see you are in a stew, but there's no need. Just calm down.'

'Not I C U, dolt,' called the witch. 'I O U – that's the spell. Just because you don't know anything about spelling – O U . . . U . . . cantankerous hyena you,' and the witch subsided onto the floor. 'You ruin everything.' And she seemed about to cry.

'You've just got the wrong kind of spell, that's all,' said Tom, a bit more confident, with the calldron between them. 'A *witch's* spell is quite, quite different. You've got the wrong menu, I expect.' And he had a look.

'I told you so, this is Sunday's menu,' he said triumphantly.

'Sonday's? Then you *are* on the menu. I told you.' And the witch was about to fly off the handle again.

'Today is Friday,' said Tom, keeping his distance. 'It's just an ordinary weekday, and you have ordinary weekday things.'

'Nothing strong?' said the witch hopefully, flexing her powerful arms again. Tom crouched down in the shadow. 'No adders ad'er 'andkerchiefs? No vipers vip'er noses?' she added wistfully.

'None of that,' said Tom even more firmly. 'You just want the common or garden witch's things, like deadly nightshade, and roots of stinkwort, and creeping henbane, and breath of puffballs, and one thousand and one dragon-flies' wings, and snail slime and cuckoo-spit, and cassowary's tails. The usual sort of thing. And peacock's eyes, if you like.'

The witch perked up no end at this. 'Peacock's I's?' she said eagerly.

But Tom was having none of that. 'There are no i's in

peacocks,' he enunciated very clearly. 'There are eyes. You must remember, this is a witch's spell.'

But the witch was oblivious and quite happy. 'Pass me the cassowary, dearie,' she said, and added, 'and tickle the toeds, will you?'

'*What* mother?' said Tom, still wary.

'Oh toads, then,' conceded the witch. 'And when I'd just got used to the old spelling, too. Write, then, let's get going.'

'Write what?' said Tom suspiciously.

'A new menu, of course,' said the witch, 'you double-toed jackassanapes monster, you.'

WOOD YOU BELIEVE IT?

Esau sawed wood. Esau Wood would saw wood! Oh the wood Wood would saw! One day Esau Wood saw a saw saw wood as no other wood-saw Wood saw would saw wood. In fact, of all the wood-saws Wood ever saw saw wood Wood never saw a wood-saw that would saw wood as the wood-saw Wood saw saw wood would saw wood. And I never saw a wood-saw that would saw wood as the wood-saw Wood saw would saw till I saw Esau Wood saw wood with the wood-saw that Wood saw saw wood.

(*Remind me to get someone else to chop the wretched stuff up next time!*)

Give us a hand with this page, will you?

FRIDAY'S BIRD – THE CASSOWARY

I wish I were a cassowary
On the plains of Timbuctoo,
For then I'd eat the missionary,
His prayer book and himbuctoo.

DOES A CASSOWARY REALLY LIVE ON THE PLAINS OF TIMBUCTOO?

NO, BUT THESE POETS WILL DO ANYTHING FOR A RHYME

Eat, Drink and Be Merry
(FOR TOMORROW WE DIET)

DUCHESS: 'Did you clean out the larder, Mildred?'
MILDRED: 'Oh, yes, my lady. And everything was delicious, thank you.'

What's yellow and stupid?
> Thick custard.

What is worse than finding a maggot in an apple?
> Finding half a maggot.

How can you divide nineteen apples absolutely equally between seven boys?
> Stew them, and measure them out very carefully.

What is flat and yellow and goes round at 33⅓ r.p.m. ?

A long-playing omelette.

What runs around Paris at midday, wrapped in a plastic bag ?

The lunch pack of Notre Dame.

Why do people preserve vegetables more now than they used to ?

Because they can.

There was a young lady of York,
Who ate pears through her ears, with a fork;
   She picked peas with her toes
   To her knees, then her nose,
Cos they'd stoppered her mouth with a cork!

What is the favourite drink of: a fat man; a poultry farmer; a sailor; and an undertaker ?

The fat man drinks stout.
The poultry farmer has a cocktail.
The sailor goes for port,
And the undertaker takes beer.

*

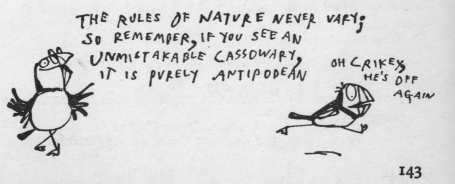

THE RULES OF NATURE NEVER VARY;
SO REMEMBER, IF YOU SEE AN
UNMISTAKABLE CASSOWARY,
IT IS PURELY ANTIPODEAN

OH CRIKEY,
HE'S OFF
AGAIN

Riddles of History Answered

The Head's Speech

If King Charles walked and talked ten minutes after his head was cut off – *what* did the head talk *about*?

If only I had looked ROUND – I wouldn't be where I am now.

*

KINGS AND QUEENS

Where did King John sign the Magna Carta?
　　At the bottom.

What was it that Queen Mary had before, and King William had behind, and Queen Anne didn't have at all ?

The letter M.

What is the name of the only king crowned in England since William the Conqueror ?

King James I. (He was King of Scotland at the time – the others weren't kings *until* they were crowned!)

Where are Kings of England usually crowned ?

On the head.

*

Riddliculous

What did the fisherman say when he caught a bus ?

'Ah, but you should have seen the one that got away!'

How can you stop a fish from smelling ?

Cut off his nose.

If cheese comes after dinner, what comes after cheese ?

A mouse.

How do you make a Swiss roll ?

Throw him down an Alp.

Have you seen what's in Friday's paper ?

Fish and chips.

Who's the fish friar's best friend ?

The chipmunk.

What zooms along the sea-bed on three wheels ?

A motor-pike and side-carp.

What sleeps at the bottom of the sea ?

A kipper.

A man was driving along in the country one day, when he saw a hare lying in the road. He got out of his car, and picked it up; it was quite lifeless, but otherwise undamaged.

Then along came a man on a motorbike, who stopped, and going to his saddlebag, took out a small bottle. He opened the hare's mouth, and poured something down it. Immediately, the hare jumped out of his hands, and ran off, lollipy, lollipy, across the fields.

'I say,' said the first man, 'what was that? Brandy?' 'No,' said the second. 'Hare-restorer.'

Jest Animals

THE HORSE THAT WON THE DERBY

A man was leaning over a gate one day, in the country, when he saw a very old horse quietly munching the grass. It was the most knock-kneed, tumble-down, moth-eaten, skinny-ribbed old horse you ever saw. The man was just thinking to himself that he'd never seen such an old junk-heap in his life, when the horse suddenly said:

'I know what you're thinking. You're thinking I'm just a rotten bag of old bones. That's what *you* think. Well, let me tell you – I may not look anything much nowadays, because I'm old. But I won the Derby. It may be a long time ago, but I promise you, when I was younger I came first – in the Derby.'

And the horse went back to munching. The man couldn't believe his ears. He waited for the horse to speak again. He called to him. But the horse didn't answer. It just went on munching as if nothing had happened.

Finally the man went on down the road, until he saw an old man, sitting outside some stables.

'I say,' said the man. 'It's the oddest thing. There's a horse down the road – and I know you won't believe it – but he spoke to me.'

'Oh aye,' said the old man. 'What did he say?'

'Well, actually,' said the man, rather taken aback, 'he said he won the Derby.'

'Ruddy liar,' said the old man. 'That horse never won the Derby – he only came second.'

*

And now, let me see, shall I tell you the one about the Taj Mahal?

No, I don't think it's up your street.

Very Mental Arithmetic

1. Supposing you have 5p. You spend 2p, and lose 3p. What have you got left in your pocket?
2. Can you take one from 19 and leave 20?

3. Long ago there was an Empress of China who was obviously a bit of a pig, because she set her pig-keeper this impossible task – and threatened to dismiss him immediately if he didn't find the answer.

   The pig-keeper had twenty-four pigs and four sties. The Empress insisted that these twenty-four pigs were so arranged in the sties that however many times she went round visiting them, she would always find the number of pigs in each sty she came to *nearer to ten* than in the sty before.

The poor man suffered terribly for some time, thinking it really was quite impossible. BUT – he found an answer. It was a bit tricky, but the Empress was satisfied. What was it?

4. What would you add to nine to make six?

Answers: Number 7 at the end of the book.

Aunt Christabel's Questions

I've had a lot of aunts, but the best was great-aunt Christabel Culpepper-Jones. She was good at lots of things – like turning cartwheels (when she was seventy), and tossing pancakes (when she was hungry).

She was also very good at asking questions, like these:
AUNT C.: 'There were two sheep standing in a field. One

was looking due North and the other due South. How could they see each other without turning round?'

AUNT C.: 'Now here's one small handkerchief. Can you lay it on the ground so that you and I can *both* stand on it, with *both* feet – without touching each other?'

AUNT C.: 'Now here's a weight – about a lb. or so. I'm going to tie it to the bottom of this string. Right? Now I'm going to hold the top of the string with one hand. And *now* – watch carefully – I'm going to cut the string in the middle – and yet the weight will not fall to the ground.'

How did she do it? (The weight must be swinging free, and you mustn't touch it – or put anything under it!)

Great-aunt Christabel was a great one for making me work things out – but don't worry – the answers are Number 8 at the end of the book.

✻

Speech Day on Friday

Professor Goodenough was the guest of honour at the annual Speech Day at Grindstone Hall. He was late in arriving, and stumbled panting on to the platform, where he adjusted his dark spectacles and stroked his flowing beard, and made the following speech.

'Ladies and Jellyspoons,
I stand upon this speech
To make a platform, which,
As I have been long, will be short.
I would like to address you today,
If you would hand up the envelopes,
On the facts of life.
These are birth and death.
And now it only remains for me
To remind you that
God is a shoving leopard to us all;
That many hands make light work,
Hence electricity;
That many lands make height work,
Hence hydro-electricity;
And in the time to come, which is before you, in the years
    ahead,
Look before you leap.'

*Whereupon he stepped off the platform and fell flat on his
face.*

No. 5 The Campfire Sausage Griller

For years the fried sausage – burnt on one side and uncooked on the other – was one of the most dangerous hazards of outdoor cookery. It became a thing of the past with the perfection of the Campfire sausage griller, the result of experiments on the South African veldt by Major-General Sir Vivian Squinch and a platoon of his men.

Do you Noah these?

How did Noah manage in the dark?
> He turned on the flood lights.

Where was Moses when the lights went out?
> Under the bed, looking for the matches.

What was Amos's second name?
> Quito.

How did Adam and Eve feel when they were expelled from the Garden of Eden?
> Very put out.

Who's the first person in the Bible?
> Chap one.

And what did the Egyptians do when the lights went out?
> They turned on the Israelites.

*

Did you think everything went into the Ark in pairs?
Well, the worms went in apples.

Four Ways of Saying The Same Thing – What?

I came from beyond the ocean,
I drank water out of the sea,
I lighten many a nation
And I give myself to thee.

What is it that
Falls down a cliff and
   doesn't break,
Falls in the water and
   doesn't sink,
Falls on the fire, and
   doesn't burn?

Hickamore, hackamore,
On the king's kitchen door.
All the king's horses
And all the king's men
Cannot drive hickamore, hackamore,
Off the king's kitchen door.

In a murky road, so I've been told,
There is a little barrel of gold.

Answer: The sun and sunbeams.

The King and the Warder's Daughter

Once upon a time there was a very wicked king who threatened to destroy an entire village, unless someone in it managed to answer three puzzles.

The villagers fetched the warder's daughter, because she was the cleverest person in the village, and sent her to the king.

'Go home,' ordered the king, 'and make me a shirt and trousers, out of only *two* threads'.

The girl went home, and then she sent the king two broomsticks. With a message. Would the king kindly make her a loom and bobbin-wheel out of them, so that she could start weaving?!

The king raged and fumed, but he couldn't do it. So he sent the girl his second puzzle. This was an earthern pot, with the bottom out. He told the girl that she must sew a bottom into the pot, so that no seam or stitch could be seen.

The girl sent back a message to the king. Would he please turn the pot inside out for her – because cobblers always sew on the *inside*, never the outside?

Well – the king raged and fumed even more, but he couldn't do it. So this time he asked the most impossible riddle of all. This time the warder's daughter must come to him – neither driving, walking, nor riding; she must be neither dressed, *nor* naked; she mustn't be out of the road *nor* in the road; and she must bring him something as a gift which was *not* a gift! With so many impossible, topsy-turvy things to do, the king was sure that this time, anyway, the girl would fail.

She didn't. She put two wasps between two plates. She stripped and wrapped herself in a fishing-net. She put her goat into the rut on the road, and with one foot on the goat's back and the other in the road she made her way to the king. There she lifted up one of the plates and the wasps flew away! So she *had* brought the king a present, and yet it wasn't a present!

Well, after all that, the king thought he could never find a cleverer woman, so he married her, and the village lived happily ever after.

(*Not only clever, but an acrobat too! If you've got a goat and a fishing-net, you can try it for yourself.*)

*

Puzzles

HOW MANY TOES HAS A PUSSYCAT?

Can you tell me why
A liar's eye
Can better see
Than you – or me
On how many toes
A pussycat goes?

The eye of deceit
Can best counterfeit,
And so, I suppose,
Can best count 'er toes.

✳

Go on
MAKE A SPECTACLE OF YOURSELF!
and read this

Words keep running through my head.

Bull rushes
Hat stands
Pub crawls
Bean stalks
Cow slips
Butter flies
Hen runs
Cat walks

Hops

Full stops

. . . .

Friday Night's Dream

There were once three men marooned on a desert island. As time went by they gradually ate up all their food, until at last they only had one thing left – a bread-roll.

Now the three men agreed that whoever had the best dream that night would have the roll to eat the next day.

So they all went to sleep and they all dreamed. And next morning they all met together, to tell their dreams.

Bert said he'd had the most fantastic dream. 'I was sitting at a table completely *covered* with food – cakes, ices, sausages, biscuits, chips, chops, everything you could think of. And I could eat just as much as I liked. There were waiters who brought me anything I wanted. And there were two more who filled up my glass whenever it was empty. I've never had such delicious food in my life. It was terrific.'

And then it was Fred's turn. He said *he'd* had the most fantastic dream, too. 'I was on a magic carpet, flying all over the world. I went right over the Himalayas and the top of Everest. I saw the polar bears at the North Pole and the penguins at the South Pole. I saw huge deserts, and herds of elephants stampeding across the plains of Kilimanjaro. I've never seen such amazing sights. It was tremendous.'

And then it was Sid's turn. He said *he'd* had the most fantastic dream, too. 'I dreamt the roll was going mouldy. So I woke up, and ate it.'
                                              *

Why didn't the monkey hurt himself when he jumped, from 2,000 feet into a glass of lemonade?

    It was a soft drink.

What's Saturday, mate?
Saturday's GREAT!
It's stay-up-late.

Saturday's
Natterday,
Eat-and-grow-fatter-day.

Saturday's
Clatter-day,
Chip chop and chatter day.

Saturday's
Scatter-day,

Never get up
Cos it don't really matter-day.

It's a that-a-day,
SATURDAY.

READ ALL ABOUT IT!

*

And now you've heard the story about the bread, shall I tell you the one about the butter? No, I'd better not – you might spread it.

NO WONDER
I GET SO
CRUSTY

THE DAILY SUCCESS
Saturday

GENERAL KNICKERBOCKER FLIES BACK TO FRONT

QUEEN'S AWARD GIVES FILLIP TO INDUSTRY

FORD CAR TALKS

A CAR CASE

An old Ford was buried yesterday, in the Park Lawn Automotive Cemetery.

At the grave site, suitably marked by a parking meter showing an 'expired' sign, the Ford was gently lowered into an enormous pit.

It all cost £12. For a few extra pence a sign will be provided that says simply: *'Rust in peace'**

Bishop Baked For Village

Meat Shortage - Housewives Attack Ministers

BARKING GOALKEEPER SENT OFF

Mr Mickey Mouse arrested

Wellington, Nov. 5. – Mr Mickey Mouse, a candidate in New Zealand's general election on November 25, was arrested here today after a Guy Fawkes day revel in the grounds of Parliament house ended in violence.

Mr Mouse, who changed his name by deed poll from Christopher Lawrence, is leader of the Mad Hatter's Tea Party and has been campaigning on a platform of free cheese.†

Ice-Cream Shop Raided Thieves Take The Lolly

TILL ROBBED OF CASH
GIRL SAYS:
I THOUGHT THE
CHANGE WOULD DO
ME GOOD

*POLICE FOUND
SAFE HIDDEN
UNDER BED*

SNAIL KILLS BULLS

**EGYPT DAM SITE
BETTER OFF
FOR U.S. FUNDS**

TURIN: A snail crept along a
power line, caused a short-
circuit, and sent a powerful
electric charge into a water
trough, killing six bulls.‡

* Daily Express   † The Times   ‡ Daily Mail

Riddleography

What do you get when you cross a bee with a bell?

A real humdinger.

What makes the Tower of Pisa lean?

It doesn't eat.

What animal is more extraordinary than a counting dog?

A spelling bee.

What happened when the gong went for dinner?

It came back – half an hour later.

Do we have blood banks in England?

No, but we have a Liverpool.

How do you make a bandstand?

Pull their chairs away.

Two oranges went rolling down a hill, but one stopped.
Why?

It ran out of juice.

What's the difference between damned souls and darned socks?

> One are dead men, and the others are men-ded.

When did London begin with an L and end with an E?

> It always began with an L, and end always began with an E.

If your friend has a whole apple, and you only have a bite, what should you do?

> Scratch it.

How far can a pirate ship go?

> Fifteen miles to the galleon.

How do you keep cool at a football match?

> Sit next to a fan.

✳

Ayes and Noes? . . . or Eyes and Nose? . . . or I's and Knows? . . .

What did the pen say to the paper?

> 'I dot my eyes on you.'

What did one eye say to the other?

> 'Something's come between us, and it smells.'

What has five eyes, but cannot see, and gets to see in the end?

> The Mississippi River.

What is it that by losing an eye, has nothing left but a nose?

> NOISE.

Where does all the pepper go?
        No one nose.

What should you always do with your eyes?
        Dot them.

*

And Toes

Moses supposes his toeses are roses,
But Moses supposes erroneously;
For nobody's toeses are posies of roses
As Moses supposes his toeses to be.

Died on Saturday

ERECTED TO THE MEMORY
OF
JAMES MACMILLAN
DROWNED IN THE RIVER SEVERN
BY SOME OF HIS CLOSEST FRIENDS

Jest Animals

Mr Smith was taking a stroll down the road one fine Monday afternoon – looking over hedges, and into gardens, admiring the roses, and seeing how everyone else's veg. were doing, when he saw a fellow, sitting on his lawn at a table, under a blue umbrella, and sitting opposite him, on a chair, was a dog. Some kind of poodle. And the man and the dog were playing chess.

Mr Smith couldn't help it. He quietly opened the garden gate, walked across the lawn, and watched. The poodle moved his bishop two squares with his paw, and sat back with a smirk on his face.

'Oh, blast it,' said the man. 'Alright. Checkmate. You win.' And he sighed and began setting up the pieces again.

Mr Smith coughed. 'Excuse me.'

'Yes?' said the man, who had been so busy with the game he hadn't noticed him.

'Excuse me,' said Mr Smith again. 'But that's the most extraordinarily clever dog you've got there. Most extraordinary. I've never seen anything like it.'

'What do you mean, clever?' said the man crossly. 'That dog's not clever. Why, that's the first time he's won, and I've beaten him three times already this morning.'

Why did little Bo-peep lose her sheep?
        She had a crook with her.
What animal would you like to be on a cold day?
        A little otter.
What animal drops from the clouds?
        The rain, dear.
Why do Swiss cows wear bells?
        Because their horns don't work.
What is white, has just one horn, and gives milk?
        A milk van.

Daft Definitions

Out of bounds	an exhausted kangaroo.
Ridiculous	an elephant hanging over a cliff, only he can't fall because his tail is tied to a daisy.
A woolly jumper	a cross between a sheep and a kangaroo.
A lemon sole	what leaves yellow footprints on the sea bed.
Air	a balloon with its skin taken off.
Metronome	a little man in the French underground.

Daft Inventions
WHO INVENTED YODELLING?

One night a man came to an inn high in the Alps, and asked for a bed. There wasn't much room, so they made up a bed for him on the landing.

The next morning the man left very early, but before he went, he stole into the rooms of the innkeeper's daughter, and his wife, and took all their jewellery. Soon after he'd gone, the innkeeper discovered that his daughter's jewellery had been taken. So he rushed out onto the mountains, shouting after the thief.

All over the mountains, the innkeeper pursued the man, calling out, 'Stop, thief,' but the man was always just too far away. At last, when the innkeeper was right on top of a mountain, he saw the man on the mountain opposite, so he called out: 'You've robbed my daughter.'

And the man yelled back: 'And your old lady, too.'

| Who invented the sword-dance? | Someone who wanted to dance and cut his toe-nails at the same time. |
| Who invented the bag-pipes? | A Scotsman who trod on his cat and liked the noise. |

Saturday's Bird: The Elephant

The elephant is a pretty bird,
It swings from bough to bough.
It makes its nest in a rhubarb-tree
And it whistles like a cow.

Haven't you heard of the elephant-bird before? Well, I bet you haven't heard of the Lesser Spotted Wobbler, or the Long-tailed Trike, either.

MORE ELEPHANTS

What did the man say when he saw four elephants coming over a hill?

'Here come four elephants.'

And what did the man say when he saw four elephants coming over a hill with dark glasses on?

Nothing. He didn't recognize them.

How do you get down from an elephant?

    You don't. You get down from a swan.

Would you rather an elephant attacked you, or a gorilla?

    I'd rather he attacked the gorilla.

Why are elephants so wrinkled?

    Have you ever tried ironing one?

Have you ever heard of a baby raised on elephant's milk?

    Yes, a baby elephant.

Why has an elephant got a trunk?

    To keep his tennis rackets in.

How do you stop a herd of elephants charging at you?

    Make a trunk call, and reverse the charge.

What do you get when you cross an elephant with a kangaroo?

    Great big holes all over Australia.

How can you tell when you're in bed with an elephant?

    By the big E on his pyjama pocket

Saturday's Poem

IT'S ALLAMING

Now, the dandies
of the
Andes,
are the
llamas,
looking
Chile,
in their
Frile,
pink pyjamas.

They pull
Caracas
with
alpacas in
Peru,
they really du,
but it's nothing –
they just
do it to
allamas.

Riddles of History Answered

What did William tell his son?

Dear Son,
   I'm so sorry I missed you yesterday. Please come home, and let me have another shot.

Your father.

✳

Why did the Romans build straight roads?

> Because they didn't want to drive their horses round the bend.

What is the difference between Noah's ark and Joan of Arc?

> One was made of wood, and the other was Maid of Orleans.

Why are the Middle Ages called the Dark Ages ?

> Because there were so many knights then.

Can you tell me of what parentage Napoleon was ?

> Of Corsican.

Why would it be better to die like Joan of Arc, than Anne Boleyn ?

> Because a hot steak is better than a cold chop.

> Caesar entered on his head,
> A helmet on each foot;
> A sandal in his strong right hand,
> A trusty sword to boot.

Nonsense !

There was once a man who was imprisoned in a cell. All around him were four solid walls. There was a solid floor and a solid ceiling, no windows, and no doors. The only thing in the room was a wooden table. How did he get out ?

Easy. He rubbed his hands together until they were sore. He took the saw and cut the table in half. Two halves make a whole. He climbed through the hole and shouted until he was hoarse. Then he jumped on the horse and rode away !

NAMING NUMEROUS NUMBERS
NUMERICALLY

One old Oxford ox obviously opening ordinary oysters;
Two tall tigers terribly tired of trying to trot to Tottenham;
Three thrifty Thanes thirstily thrusting through thorny
    thickets;

Four fat friars fanning fainting flies furiously;
Five fancy Frenchmen foolishly fishing for frogs;
Six super sportsmen savagely shooting snipes;
Seven Severn salmon secretly swallowing swimming shrimps;
Eight earnest Englishmen eagerly examining Eastern excavations;
Nine nimble noblemen nibbling nutty nougat;
Ten tinkers tinkling upon ten tin tinder-boxes with ten tenpenny tacks;
Eleven elementary elephants elegantly elevating egg-cups;
Twelve typographical topographers typically translating types;
Thirteen . . .

HELP! Now I reckon it's *your* turn – *please.*
O.K. Billions of bilious bumblebees busy barricading bereaved bandicoots with bags of benevolent blockbusters.

MISSING

Someone stole all the pennies last night, from the Olde Wishing Well.
Police are hoping for the return of the missing coppers.

PLEASE HELP THE POLICE – WITH PUNCTUATION

Jones, Smith, and Brown were Police Constables, and Brown sent this note into the Inspector one day.
   "Jones where Smith had had had had had had had had had had had the Inspector's approval."
   What does it mean, if anything?

A. *Jones, where Smith had had 'had', had had 'had had'.
Had 'had had' had the Inspector's approval ? !*

One of the mirrors is missing from the Crazy Hall of
Mirrors at the Amusement Park. It is a magnifying
mirror, and makes everyone appear larger than life.
A small force of policemen are looking into it.

Mick and Mulligan

MICK: Hey, Mulligan, have you heard about the
lion that was right down at the bottom of a
steep valley? The mountains were quite
sheer up to the sky all round, without a gap
between them. How do you think he got
there?

MULLIGAN: Sure, and he must have parachuted down,
Mick.

MICK: He didn't need the parachute, boyo. He just floated down, 'cos he was a dandelion.

MICK: And what about the bird who wanted to get a worm, but it was on the other side of a large patch of oil. Now, did that bird fly over it, hop over it, or walk through it, Mulligan?

MULLIGAN: He flew, Mick.

MICK: No he waded through it. After all, it's de oily boid dat catches de worm.

MULLIGAN: And that's logical, Mick, so it is.

MICK: Did you know, Mulligan, that in darkest Africa there are spiders that are so big that

they sit on logs and bark as people go by and
a good many of them weigh a pound!

MULLIGAN: I don't believe it!

MICK: Ah, to be sure, and it's true, I'm telling you.
They sit on the logs and bark, and a good
many of them together would weigh a pound.

What Is It?

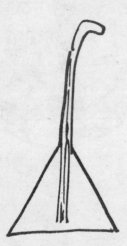

If this is a sitar

What's this?

A baby-sitar.

Long, slim, dark fellow,
Pull his tongue,
And hear him bellow.
   a gun

Short, round fat fellow,
Pull a string,
And see him yellow.
   a light bulb

Crooked as a rainbow,
Teeth like a cat,
I bet a gold fiddle,
You can't guess that!
   a bramble

What is long and slim,
Works in the light,
Has but one eye,
And an awful bite?
   a needle

177

USEFUL INVENTIONS OF DAYS GONE BY

No. 6 Lightfoot's Clockwork Roller Skates

A Boon to Travellers, and suitable for Young and Old alike. Miss Elsie Grommett (at right), is holder of the Land's End to John O'Groats clockwork roller-skating speed and endurance record

If aeroplanes have aerodromes, and hippo's have happy homes
in hippodromes, what are

Palindromes ?

Here's a PALINDROME: Able was I ere I saw Elba.

It's very famous – someone made it up for Napoleon, after he was dead.

The trick isn't at all easy. You have to make a sentence that means exactly the same whether you read it coming or going, backwards or forwards.

Like the first thing Adam said to Eve:

Madam, I'm Adam.

(There's no Introduction in the Bible, so I suppose he had to.)

Here are two more – pretty rotten ones, on account of its being such a difficult thing to do:

Repel evil as a live leper.

Stop, Rose, I prefer pies or pots!

If you want to have a go – here are a few words which may come in handy, because of their good back-to-frontness.

level, revel, noon, was, ton, meet

THIS IS A DROODLE

Guess what ?

A duck drinking out of a bucket.

Real Puzzlers – 2

You have to have a bit of the old grey matter to get to the bottom of these!

1. How can a woman have five children, and yet exactly half of them are boys?

2. A big Indian and a little Indian were walking down the road. The little Indian was the son of the big Indian, yet the big Indian was not the father of the little Indian. Why?

3. An old cowboy had two sons, and when he died, he left all his money to whichever son was the *last* to ride his horse out of the stable gate, into the fields. Each son had a horse – and each son kept his horse in the stable day after day. Neither wanted to take his horse out first – so it was deadlock, and no one moved. Finally a tramp came along, and gave them some advice. Then the sons jumped on the horses and raced for the gate. What advice did the tramp give?

4. A man was going to Brighton, when he lost his way. At last he came to a main road. There were no sign-posts, but two men were standing there.

   The trouble was, one of them always told the truth, and the other man always lied; but which was which, the traveller didn't know.

   He found out the right way to go by asking only *one* question of only *one* man. How was that?

Answers: Number 9 at the end of the book.

*

Part of a Riddle Ballad

Once, long ago, there were three sisters, who were all in love with the same knight. The youngest was so keen, that she kept on and on asking him to marry her, until at last the knight answered:

'If thou canst answer me questions three
This very day will I marry thee.'

'Kind sir, in love,' O then quoth she,
'Tell me what your three questions be.'

'Oh what is longer than the way,
Or what is deeper than the sea?

'Or what is louder than the horn,
Or what is sharper than the thorn?

'Or what is greener than the grass,
Or what is worse than a woman was?'

'O love is longer than the way,
And hell is deeper than the sea.

'And thunder is louder than the horn,
And hunger is sharper than a thorn.

'And poison is greener than the grass,
And the Devil is worse than woman was.'

When she these questions answered had,
The knight became exceeding glad.

And after, as it is verified,
He made of her his lovely bride.

So now, fair maidens all, adieu,
This song I dedicate to you.

I wish that you may constant prove,
Unto the man that you do love.

(*I make it* six *questions, actually – but I suppose it wouldn't rhyme with 'thee'.*)

And an Old Riddle Song

I HAD FOUR BROTHERS

1. I had four brothers over the sea,
   And they each sent a present unto me,

2. The first sent a goose without any bone,
   The second sent a cherry without any stone.

3. The third sent a blanket without any thread,
   The fourth sent a book than no man could read.

4. How could there be a goose without any bone?
   How could there be a cherry without any stone?

5. How could there be a blanket without any thread?
   How could there be a book that no man could read?

6. When the goose is in the egg, it has no bone,
   When the cherry's in the blossom, it has no stone.

7. When the wool's on the sheep, it has no thread,
   When the book is in the press, no man can it read.

The Battle of Waterloo was won on the playing fields of Eton (so they say).

A very special Match of the Day report

By extraordinary good luck, we have found an old recording of this historic match. A lot of the tape has been destroyed over the years, so here are a few extracts which remain. Your commentator is Lord Colman. We take up the game at extra-time.

'And so, with the score standing at 18,258 all, this tremendous match goes into extra-time. And here comes Wellington now, leading his team back onto the field for this historic match, England and the Rest of Europe, versus France. And what a magnificent sight the English look in their red and gold colours. And now here are the French, in their all blue strip – I can't see Napoleon at the moment – yes, there he is, taking up a defensive position, at the back of the field.

And they're off! – they're away – and the ball is out on the wing – the English are tearing up the field in attack, they're bombarding the French – and there's a shot now – What a shot – but the French have turned it away – the French have got the advantage now, they're past the Germans – the Dutch are coming in to block them, but the French have swerved, they're making for the goal, the English are nowhere. Oh! that was close. What a muddle in the defence. Ney for France has got complete command of the mid-field. They're shooting from every angle – and Ney has got a head to it – but Wellington is there – it's just off the line – Yes – Wellington has got it away . . .

What a close finish – still no further score, and England are being hard pressed. Can they pull this out of the bag at the eleventh hour? There's very little time left for play now – and England are bringing on the Prussian – they're bringing on Blucher! Can he do it, or is it too late? And Blucher is making all the difference. Wellington is rallying his men again. The Rest of Europe and England are on the attack again . . .

And now the French are pulling the Old Guard out of defence and throwing them into the attack – the French are making a tremendous effort – but it's no good – Blucher is through, he's gone right down the French right wing – and Napoleon can't stop him – he's there – and it's a goal! Blucher has scored! . .

And Napoleon has been sent off! The captain has been sent off! – I can't quite see – there's some dispute – but he's going anyway – was it hands – no, it can't be, unless it was his left – and now the whole team are going off – France is leaving the field! The referee has called the game off. So England and the Rest of Europe have won. What a *tremendous* victory – snatched in extra-time – we'll just show you those last few hours again in slow motion. And the French are running off the field, pursued by the Prussian – and now all the Prussians are after them . . .

And here comes Wellington now, just in your picture, and the rest of his great team. For those of you with colour, you can see from the blood what a really hard match this has been – a historic match. And there's the pitch, now – my goodness, they've made a mess of that. I think the Eton groundsman will have something to say about that.'

Don't Miss This Page – It's Indispensable*

Everyone dat's in their senses
Keeps der bulls
In pens and fences.

*In dis pen's a bull.

＊

The Rary

There was once an explorer exploring down the Amazon, who found a strange little insect. It was red, and a bit squishy, with lots of legs. He'd never seen it before, so he put it in a matchbox, to keep it. Next morning, when he looked at the matchbox, the Thing had grown so much it had pushed the box open and its legs were coming out. So the explorer put it in a cardboard box, and went on down the Amazon on his raft.

And the Thing kept on growing. It doubled in size, and then it doubled again. He put it in a bigger box, and then a bigger box . . . Finally, when the explorer got down to the coast, the raft could hardly float, it was so weighted down by the Thing, all big and red and squishy, with lots of legs.

He took a boat back to Southampton, and put the Thing in a huge packing-case on deck. And the Thing kept on growing. It got bigger and redder and squishier, and its legs got longer and longer, until gradually it spread all over the deck, and the explorer and the captain and all the crew had to stay below. The explorer was in despair.

He telegraphed to a world-famous professor, an entomologist, who met them at the docks. The entomologist was delighted. 'That's a very rare thing you've got there, very rare,' he said. 'Now I've seen a blue one before, but I've never seen a red one. Most interesting.' 'What *is* it?' said the explorer. 'Oh, don't you know,' said the professor. 'It's a Rary.' 'Well, how can I get rid of it?' said the explorer. 'I must get rid of it.'

'Well, there's only one thing to do,' said the professor. 'You'll have to take it to the summit of Everest, and tip it off the top.' 'Oh no,' groaned the explorer. 'Do I really have to go that far?' 'It's the only way to get rid of a Rary,' said the professor. So that was that.

The explorer sailed to India, in a bigger boat. He got hundreds of elephants to drag the Rary to the Himalayas. He got thousands of Sherpas to carry it up to the top of Everest. He was just about to tip the great big red squishy Thing off the top, when he noticed it was heaving and shaking all over. The Rary was giggling. 'And *what's* so funny?' said the explorer.

'I was just thinking,' said the Rary. 'It's a long way to Tipperary.'

✳

And there's a very good story about the Channel Tunnel – but I don't think you'd dig it.

188

AND THEN....
SUNDAY

HEY! WAKE UP! DON'T YOU WANT TO KNOW THE

Answers

Number 1

THE CASE OF THE EIGHT STOLEN WATCHES

The thief was a punctual octopus. Sergeant Duffer caught him at Waterloo Station telephoning T I M to check up on the right time. (Actually he was in *three* telephone boxes, just to make sure.)

Number 2

THE MYSTERY OF THE MONK'S COLD FEET

A blanket is always more than a yard *wide*. So when the monk had cut a yard off, he sewed it on to the bottom of the blanket *the other way round* – and covered his feet.

Number 3

MENTAL ARITHMETIC (VERY!)

1. Two, and one to carry.
2. One haystack.
3. An eye.
4. (a) Bill and Ben went to the Bank of England on New Year's Day. Bill stood in front of it, while Ben went round and stood behind it.
   (b) All the 'nothings' they borrowed and stole, etc., are added on to the £1,000, making £1,000,000,000.

Number 4

GOLD'N FEATHERS

1. Quite true. Gold is weighed in Troy weight, which has only 12 ounces to the pound.
2. Quite true. Troy weight has 480 grains per ounce, but avoirdupois weight, in which feathers are weighed, has only 437½ grains.
3. Not *quite* true – a featherweight is between 112 and 126 lbs. (in boxing!).

Number 5

THE RIDDLE OF THE IVORY WALKING-STICKS

The thieves were the Three Blind Mice.

Sergeant Duffer said he reckoned their mum must have helped them, thinking the white sticks would be useful.

'Why not the father?' I asked. 'Oh well,' he said, 'I thought as how their dad would just have said, those kids don't need sticks, let them manage – so it would have been up to the mum.'

Number 6
REAL PUZZLERS – 1
1. How do you pronounce YES?
2. Are you asleep? (Or are you dead – or stone-deaf?)
3. Four. (The father and mother were brother and sister, one having a son, and the other a daughter.)
4. The letter E.
5. First he takes the chicken. Then he takes the wheat and brings *back* the chicken. Then he takes the fox. Finally he comes back again and collects the chicken.
6. You imagined the duck *in* the bottle? Then imagine it *out*! (Sorry about that!)

Number 7
VERY MENTAL ARITHMETIC
1. A hole.
2. Take I from XIX and leave XX.
3. The pig-keeper put 8 pigs in the first sty; 10 in the second; 0 in the third, and 6 in the fourth (10 is nearer ten than 8; 0 is nearer ten than 10 – that's the tricky bit; 6 is nearer ten than nothing; and 8 is nearer ten than 6). Horrible, isn't it? But this is another of Lewis Carroll's riddles, and that was just the sort of thing he did.
4. Add S to IX to make SIX.

Number 8
AUNT CHRISTABEL'S QUESTIONS
1. The sheep were facing each other!
2. Put the handkerchief on the floor, in the doorway, so that half is one side of the door, and then shut it. You can't possibly touch someone with the door between you.
3. Tie a loop in the string – and then cut the loop. It's easier if you get someone else to hold the string – then you have both hands for tying.
(These are *very good* for trying on someone else!)

Number 9
REAL PUZZLERS – 2
1. All of them were boys!

2. She was his mother.
3. The tramp told his two sons to ride each other's horse.
4. He asked *either* man: 'If I ask the other man the way to Brighton which direction will he say?' Then he takes the opposite way.

And if you've enjoyed this book, you might try ...

Bricks and Mortar – by Bill Ding
Welsh Roads – by Dai Version
All About Explosives – by Dinah Mite
How to Make Wrought Iron – by Ida Black-Smith
Schoolboy Jokes – by R. T. Lafter
The Chinese Week – by Fri-Sat Sun
My Days in China – by Sun Mon Tue

... and you'll certainly enjoy

Little Red Record Book – *Bronnie Cunningham*
Codes for Kids – *Burton Albert Jnr*
The Puffin Book of Athletics – *Neil Allen*
All the Year Round – *Toni Arthur*
My Secret File – *John Astrop*
Deeper Secrets – *John Astrop*
Johnny Ball's Think Box – *Johnny Ball*
Plays for Laughs – *Johnny Ball*
The Puffin Book of Car Games – *Douglas St P. Barnard*
You Can do the Cube – *Patrick Bossert*
Micro Games – *Patrick Bossert & Philippa Dickinson*
The Puffin Crossword Puzzle Book – *Alan Cash*
The Crack-a-Joke Book
Card Games for Children – *Len Collis*
Go! A Book of Games – *Philippa Dickinson*
The Puffin Book of Brainteasers – *Eric Emmet*
The Puffin Book of Football – *Brian Glanville*
Houdini's Book of Magic – *Ben Hamilton*
How to Survive – *Brian Hildreth*
The Big Book of Puzzles – *Ronald Ridout and Michael Holt*
The Puffin Book of Magic – *Norman Hunter*
Cooking is a Game you Can Eat – *Fay Maschler*
Test Your Memory – *Adrian Sington*

(because they are real books published by PUFFINS*)*